"Thanks to Rory  who love animals but .... help them now have an all-inclusive guide to being their savior."

—Russell Simmons

"Passionately argued, tender, and harrowing . . . Ready to make love an action verb? *Beg* is your essential handbook."

—Lisa Bloom, *New York Times* bestselling author of
Think and *Swagger*

"I can honestly say that Rory has done more than any other person I know to promote the cause of compassion for animals. . . . *Beg* is a vital piece of literature . . . "

—John Joseph, lead singer of the Cro-Mags

"Funny and heartwarming, but also revealing, *Beg* is a must-read for every animal lover."

—Emily Deschanel, actress and activist

"*Beg* is an important book to read for anyone who cares about animals. Rory manages to educate, inspire, and entertain all at once. I BEG you to read it."

—Dr. Jenn Berman, host of VH1's *Couples Therapy*

"If you love your dog or cat, if you love animals, this book is a must. You will be talking about it for years, because it will change your life and make you a better person."

—John Robbins, bestselling author *Diet For A New America*, *The Food Revolution*, and co-founder of The Food Revolution Network

"Funny and frank. Ms. Freedman . . . lays it on the line with her unembarrassed love for the dogs in her own life and a perfect plan as to how every dogophile can shake a leg to help dogs and other living beings."

—Ingrid Newkirk, co-founder and president PETA (People for the Ethical Treatment of Animals)

"This book will show you how to be an irresistibly happy person whose own life has the power to uplift the whole world."

—Sharon Gannon, co-founder of Jivamukti Yoga

"Rory Freedman heard the call of billions of suffering animals and was brave enough to answer it in print, in the media, and in your face."

—Simone Reyes, animal rights activist and cast member of *Running Russell Simmons*

"*Beg* has all the wit and no-pulled-punches style of *Skinny Bitch*, and Rory Freedman's intensely personal revelations will tug at your heart at the same time that you are chuckling at her candor."

—Alexandra Paul, actress and activist

"With writing so crisp, honest, and engaging, you won't put this book down—at least not until it's time to walk the dog."

—Victoria Moran, bestselling author of *Main Street Vegan* and *Creating a Charmed Life*

". . . . Your eyes will be opened, but more importantly, so will your heart."

—Nathan Runkle, executive director Mercy for Animals

"The message is contagious—an amazing example of advocacy."

—Tatiana von Furstenburg, filmmaker

"*Beg* is an important book. . . . It asks us to step up in awareness and begin making more conscious choices in our daily lives. Thank you, Rory, for the wake-up call."

—Ben Lee, award winning singer/songwriter, actor

"*Beg* makes the process of changing our relationship to animals feel easy and inspired rather than burdensome."

—Ione Skye, actress, painter, and director

"In *Beg*, like in *Skinny Bitch*, Rory Freedman explains directly and succinctly about how each of us can make simple choices to create a better world. Kindness to animals is good for animals, and it's also good for us. Highly recommended."

—Gene Baur, president and co-founder of Farm Sanctuary

"Rory Freedman is on a mission not just to change our lives or the lives of our companions but to make the world a better place for all its inhabitants."

—Nellie McKay, award-winning singer/songwriter and actress

"This beautiful book weaves the author's personal story with individual and universal stories of animals in our world today. I want to put a copy in the hands of everyone I know!"

—Gretchen Ryan, internationally renowned artist

"A searing exposé into the treatment of all sentient beings."

—Frances Fisher, actress and activist

Beg

A RADICAL NEW WAY OF
REGARDING ANIMALS

....

RORY FREEDMAN

RUNNING PRESS
PHILADELPHIA · LONDON

ISBN 978-0-7624-4954-5
Library of Congress Control Number: 2013933358

E-book ISBN 978-0-7624-4956-9

9   8   7   6   5   4   3   2   1
Digit on the right indicates the number of this printing

Design by Joshua McDonnell
Edited by Jennifer Kasius
Typography: Avenir, and Love Ya Like A Sister

Running Press Book Publishers
2300 Chestnut Street
Philadelphia, PA 19103-4371

Visit us on the web!
www.runningpress.com

CONTENTS

For the animals. All of them.

··

(And in honor of the people who make
the world a better place for them.)

"... it is the fate of many wild creatures either to be unwanted by man or wanted too much, despised as a menace to progress or desired as a means to progress—beloved and brutalized all at once. ..."

—MATTHEW SCULLY, *Dominion*

"*Although the world is full of suffering, it is also full of the overcoming of it.*"

—HELEN KELLER

INTRODUCTION

I find it fascinating. We're all out in the world, wearing clothes, carrying things, driving cars. We encounter other humans and sum up one another based on what we see. But we totally forget that many of these humans have animals at home. That one of the biggest parts of who they are isn't immediately apparent to the outside world. Like a secret life. Sometimes I'm out, dressed cute, talking to people, being social. And they have no idea that at home, there are three dogs who are madly in love and totally obsessed with me. And that even though I'm having a good time, in the back of my mind, my dog clock is ticking, carefully calculating the number of hours since they last peed or pooped, and how long we've been away from each other. Sure, there are times I'm having so much fun, I'm bummed I need to leave to go take care of my dogs. But I'm usually eager to get back to my brood—my family. The three hairy aliens I live with are my favorite beings on the planet. I have dear, beloved friends I love so much it hurts. I have human kin I adore. But the truth is, there is no one I love like my dogs.

For me, so much of it is physical. I kiss them full on, right smack in the center of their perfect little mouths. I habitually bite them—the tips of their ears, the tops of their ears, the sides of their lips, their elbows, their toes, their nails, their paws, their backs, their necks, their throats, those bones underneath and to the sides of their chins. I pat their chests, bellies, and butts to a cadence I can feel in my soul. I pull their teeth (gently, just a little—just the big ones). I pinch them; I grab their legs when they walk by; I push them; I pull them; I manually wag their tails; I tease them; I body slam them (not really, but you know what I mean); I put them into my own version of a half nelson; I spoon them; I hug them; I squeeze them; I devour them; and I inhale them. They are completely intoxicating. Blindfolded, I could pick their individual breaths out of a lineup, should the need or a contest ever arise. For the most part, I can read their thoughts and anticipate their needs. And when I can't, I'm unsettled, because all I want is for them to be happy.

I'm just like all the other dog-loons out there who feel exactly the same about their fur-spring. We buy them toys; we buy them beds; we buy them collars and leashes and harnesses; and sometimes we buy them clothes. We talk about them too much—sometimes to other dog people who care (*read:* people who patiently wait for you to stop so they can then talk about their dogs), sometimes to nondog people who don't. We talk in stupid voices, and we say stupid things. We get into fights with other dog-loons at dog parks; we gossip about those who are too strict with their dogs and those who aren't strict enough; and we behave just like the insecure, neurotic parents of human children who want their kids to be included.

Some of us dogaphiles are cat-crazy, too. And some of us even have strong feelings for animals we've never met. While it may not be that obsessive love we have for our own children, we care deeply about the animals of the world. They may not be as cute, cuddly, accessible, or relatable as our dogs, but we recognize their capacity to feel. And in this recognition, our own humanity is reflected back at us. This book is a love letter to all animals and a celebration of their amazingness.

But most of all, this book is a call to arms to my fellow animal lovers to be *better* animal lovers. It's an invitation to be more than just good parents to the cats and dogs we live with; *Beg* is a battle cry to wake up and rise up on behalf of the world's animals.

CHAPTER 1

ALL MY CHILDREN

L ike every other psychotic dog mom, I could write an entire book about my pack. I adopted the first two, Timber and Joey, in 2000 with my then boyfriend, Reggie. (Reggie isn't his real name. In order to protect his privacy, I'm using the name of his first dog.)

Timber is a yellow Lab and, quite frankly, gorgeous. My friends Ari and Mikko call him "the Brad Pitt of dogs" (and they've actually met the human Brad Pitt). Timber is the boss of me and the other dogs; he's the director of kitchen operations; and he's in charge of all the toys in the house. He's a great white shark, a polar bear, and brontosaurus. (Don't ask me to explain this. Just know it.)

Joey, his sister and littermate, is a black Lab. (Isn't is interesting that dogs in the same litter can be totally different colors?) She's got bedroom eyes and is big on eye contact, which can be endearing and disconcerting at the same time. While Timber would be happy on a couch eating bonbons all day, Joey is an outdoorsy kinda girl. She's sporty, very *Call of the Wild*. If she ever had to go it alone, she'd not only be fine, she'd be happy. Joey's a kangaroo, a bat, a monkey, and a mosquito.

Timber and Joey are both dreamy. Seriously. And they have great senses of humor. Reggie and I were certain we knew exactly what the dogs' voices would sound like if they could talk (a mixture of shrill and scratchy) and what they would say (they're disrespectful but ultimately obedient, funny, and they swear a lot). We would constantly talk as the dogs. So clearly, Reggie was (and still is) as obsessed with the dogs as I am. But one night, out with friends, he pulled me aside to tell me I was talking about the dogs too much and I was boring everyone. *Mortifying.* But despite that embarrassment, many times after that I observed myself doing it again. I couldn't stop. Everything Timber and Joey did was cute and funny and interesting and silly and precious and wonderful and adorable and perfect. Okay, the time they turned a hotel room's two Yellow Pages into confetti while we were at a wedding may not qualify as "wonderful" or "perfect." And there was nothing "precious" about the destruction of an entire queen-size bed (mattress and box spring), the chewing of walls and floors, the jumping out windows (first floor) and hopping over fences, or the countless times they peed and pooped in the house. But I do think the Thanksgiving when Timber scarfed down an apple pie made by Reggie's cousin, who was nine months pregnant and had stayed up all night using this little lattice-making tool that some relative of theirs had smuggled out of a war-torn country a century or two ago, makes for a good story. (The cousin cried when she saw the pie remnants. *Sorry, Amy.*)

"Precious," "perfect," and "wonderful"? Who am I kidding? My dogs were evil. Pure evil. Everyone we encountered who had Labs would say,

"Yeah, it takes them about two years to outgrow the destructive phase." It took ours about six years to stop being wild maniacs. But they're my wild maniacs, and I love them so much it makes my teeth hurt. Speaking of teeth, one time, when we were hiking, Timber had a sneezing fit. He sneezed so many times and with such force, he banged his snout on the ground and broke off one of his big fangs. Ugh, see? I can't stop myself. And I haven't even mentioned little Lucy yet and all the ridiculousness she brings to the table. Lucy is my third, "late-in-life" baby.

Reggie and I had long since parted ways, on good terms. Since we adopted Timber and Joey together and since we both loved the dogs, it was never a question of "who would get the dogs" but "how should we share custody so that it works best for all of us." In Los Angeles, summer and the surrounding months can be pretty hot, and hiking trails can be riddled with poisonous rattlesnakes. In Northern California, where Reggie and his beautiful wife Gina live, winter and the surrounding months can bring so many feet of snow, it's hard for the dogs to even walk. So as a post-nuclear family, we decided Reggie and Gina would take the dogs for six months and then I'd take them for six months. My jet-setting hooligans summer in Northern Cali and winter in LA. Not a bad life.

Twice a year, I meet up with Reggie and Gina at a park between LA and Northern Cali. We hang out for an hour or so while the dogs run around and splash in the creek. Then, the dogs jump into the car of whoever they haven't been with the past six months, and off they go. People marvel at this. The three of us can't imagine doing it any other way. I mean, we get that it's unusual, but it's pretty awesome. Reggie and Gina like to snowboard and ski in the winters, and this way, they can be on the slopes for hours without worrying about rushing home to the dogs. I like to travel in the summers, and I love feeling like I can roam the globe knowing my dogs couldn't possibly be in better hands. Reggie and Gina are Timber and Joey's parents, too, and they're the only people on the planet who love them as much as I do and know them as well. (By the way, Gina is a pseudonym, too. I texted her to find out her first pet's name. It was a dog named Jason. But Gina was a subsequent pet name so I went with it. She also had mice named Pip and Squeak, but I thought referring to her by one of those names might be distracting.) Sharing custody is such an awesome set-up, we think everyone should do it. Yes, there are times we miss the dogs. But we text and email each other pictures, videos, and updates, and there are always other people's dogs around to love on when you feel a pang.

In the summer of 2010, the dogs were living it up with their other parents, and I was living it up preparing for a monthlong trip to Peru. My friend Jane Garrison sent an email out asking if someone would please help *foster* a dog for a week or two. (Just like in the human world, fostering means that you take care of the animal temporarily, until a full-time adoption takes place.) God bless Jane and all she does for animals. In addition to a million other things, she regularly pulls ten dogs at a time from *open admission* shelters, and then finds them foster homes or forever homes. (*Open admission* shelters are shelters that euthanize animals if they can't get them adopted within a certain period of time.) On this rescue round, Jane had already placed eight of the ten dogs with a foster mom who had a great track record for finding dogs forever homes. The other two couldn't be placed with the pack because they had kennel cough, which is contagious, and Jane and her husband were going out of town so they couldn't take care of them themselves. Since my dogs were away, I was more than happy to help foster a dog or two temporarily, just until I had to leave for

Peru. It would feel good to be helpful, and I was in need of a doggie fix.

The next day, Jane brought over Rose. Rose was a shaved little Muppet with white hair and a pink body underneath. Her ears and tail and pink pig belly were scabbed over from fleabites, and if you looked closely, you could see she was missing a bottom tooth. (I later learned she was missing more than one.) She had already bonded with Jane in the few days Jane had her, but she was scared of me. My heart broke for this raggedy little angel. She was an *owner surrender* at the shelter, meaning the human who was her parent had abandoned her there. Even though she seemed like such an innocent baby, herself, she had obviously had puppies at least once. I don't know if she was a breeding dog someone had used to make money or if she just came from a neglected home, but she acted like she had never been outside before. She had never seen a mirror, stairs, doors, or cars. She'd never been on a walk.

For the next few days, I did everything I could to take care of Rose and make her feel safe and secure—I gave her a ton of treats, brushed what was left of her shaved white coat, gently and slowly de-scabbed her ears and tail, and took her to the vet. She had fleas, worms, and kennel cough, all of which the vet treated. I spoke quietly and gently to her; I didn't scold her when she had an accident inside; and I let her dictate how physically close she wanted to be to me. I also changed her name. She didn't respond to Rose at all, and I wanted her to have a new beginning and new association with her new life.

I was walking her one morning, and she was being so gentle and good (as opposed to Timber and Joey who would drag me around like two pulling maniacs). I thought, "Whoever gets this dog is going to be so lucky. She is going to be *the light* of their lives. *La luz.* (*La luz* is "the light" in Spanish.) Lucy." Lucy. It just seemed to fit her. And, truth be told, I thought it was exactly the kind of name that would appeal to someone who likes little, white, foofy dogs. I'd sucker some LA glamour-puss into adopting her with a name like Lucy.

It didn't take long for Lucy to fall madly in love with me. I, on the other hand, had zero intention of adopting a third dog, and did everything I could to keep a safe emotional distance from her. I honestly didn't think it would be hard. My setup with Reggie and Gina was perfect, and my life was clearly mapped out where dogs were concerned. So I did all the things one does when trying to find a forever home for a dog. I posted her on Petfinder.com. I posted her on my Facebook page. I emailed all my friends and asked them to help spread the word. Through referrals, an elderly woman came to meet Lucy one day, as did a young couple. But somehow, as lovely as they were, it didn't seem like the right fit. This dog was the sweetest, gentlest girl I had ever met in my life; it had to feel completely right.

Throughout this process, Jane and I spoke daily. As busy as she is being a hero, Jane takes the time to deal with the psychological fallout her foster parents experience. Every time I'd tell Jane something Lucy had done or progress she made, she'd say, "Wow, she's so attached to you. . . ." And every time I'd cut her off: "Jane, not a chance. Timber and Joey aren't into other dogs; they'd be totally irked if they had to share me; they'd eat all her food; it's not even possible to walk three dogs at once; Lucy needs to be the apple of her mommy's eye, and I already have two apples; and what would I do with her when I traveled? It's not happening."

This went on and on for two or three weeks. But after the first week and a half, there were a few chinks in my armor. Jane started telling me about some other friends who had gone through the same thing and how well it worked out. And how she had the perfect pet sitters who could come stay with Lucy at my place while I went backpacking in Peru. And the clincher: how she felt bad for Lucy since she was obviously so attached to me. I had been bringing Lucy with me everywhere so she wouldn't be home alone thinking she'd been abandoned by another human.

I even brought her to my therapy appointment. (It wasn't lost on me that I had become a dog-toting LA girl with a little white frou-frou named Lucy.) At the beginning of the session, Lucy had been more independent and less scared than she'd ever been. Instead of trying to sit on my lap, she positioned herself on the other end of the sofa, with her butt facing me, and she just hung out. It was unprecedented. I don't remember if Lucy did something else unusual or not, or what prompted my therapist to say it, but at one point she said, "She's a therapy dog. She knows exactly what you need." I was blubbering, but coherent enough to marvel at the possibility. This dopey little Muppet had peed on my dining room table, could not figure out the concept of doors (she still struggles with this two and a half years later), and didn't immediately recognize me when I came back from the rare occasion I had to leave her home alone. A therapy dog? My friend James endearingly but seriously refers to her as "the dumbest dog in the world."

I left therapy and called a friend while driving home. I don't know what happened that night, but between my therapy session and that phone call, something shifted. Where before there was fear and doubt and logistical impossibility, there was now an overriding sense of wanting to be of service to this creature. It outweighed all my reasons for why it was a bad idea. I kept thinking of the expression "throw your hat over the wall." Initially, you may not know how you're going to scale the giant wall in front of you, but once you throw your hat over, you have to figure it out one way or another. Still in the car, I called, Jane crying hysterically, hyperventilating, barely able to talk: "We're suppooooosed to be togeeeeeether.

Lucy and I are meant for each ooooother." And that was it. Lucy was mine and I was hers. I'm the jerk who got stuck with the foofy white dog with the foofy white dog name. Perfect.

A day or two later, I had this nagging "buyer's remorse" and was filled with doubt about my decision. I was driving east on Melrose and saw this big, white, hunky pit bull, who was so much more my type. I thought, sadly, "I'll never have him; I went and blew my third dog pick on little bunny foo-foo." I shared my feelings with Jane, who assured me that my sentiment was totally normal and part of the process, and that it would go away. And of course, she was right. Today, Lucy is not the only one madly in love. The feeling is mutual, and I do believe we were meant for each other. As dumb as she is (and let me tell you, she is *really* dumb), she's taught me so much. And she's wormed her way into my heart. She's a white wiggle worm. And a chicken worm. And a bucking bronco. (Depending on the hair day she's having, she can also look like a Chinese luck dragon or Falkor from that '80s movie, *The NeverEnding Story*. It's true. I'm not just being a stage mom—other people say it all the time.)

In a speech I once gave at Animal Acres, a farm animal sanctuary forty miles from LA, I told the story of Lucy and Jane Garrison. I joked about being a "foster failure" and how I got "Garrisoned." A bunch of people in the crowd started nodding their heads; they too had been Garrisoned. Jane has rescued thousands of dogs from death through sheer tenacity, passion, and determination. Many years ago, there was a photo on the cover of *People* magazine of the doctor who successfully developed the science of "test tube" babies. He was surrounded by all the children he had brought into the world. I always think of Jane this way, surrounded by all the dogs she's saved. My little Lucy is just one of them.

CHAPTER 2

BASIC MATH + UNINFORMED PEOPLE = A BUNCH OF DEAD DOGS AND CATS

L ucy came from a shelter in Southern California, and the day she got pulled, 180 dogs were euthanized. One hundred and eighty. Just that day. In just that shelter.

In the United States alone, it's estimated that anywhere between six and eight million animals enter shelters every year. And that three to four million are euthanized. Every year. It's so easy to tsk and cluck and shake your head at the number. I'm doing it myself as I type, like a Jewish nana. Can any of us even begin to fathom that number? What it might look like, or feel like to see that many dead dogs and cats heaped in a pile? We certainly don't want to imagine it, something so unpleasant. But it's a grim reality and it happens every single year.

How? Why? It's simple math, really: Animals are breeding and being bred at a higher rate than they're being adopted. Some of the animals in shelters are strays who haven't been neutered or spayed, and are caught by Animal Control or concerned citizens. But half of the animals who enter the shelter system come from human families who no longer want them or can no longer keep them.[1] Half! Here's what happens: John Jones wants a dog. He buys a German shepherd from a breeder whose ad he sees online somewhere. Three years later, he has to relocate for a job. And the prized puppy he couldn't wait to have, who he shelled out $1,500 for, is no longer shiny and new. Instead of figuring out a way to take his dog with him (there's always a way), he makes a feeble, half-hearted attempt to find the dog a new home. It doesn't work, so he drops the dog off at a shelter, even knowing that if the dog isn't adopted, he will be killed.

Susan Smith's children have been bugging her for a dog for years. One day, at the mall, she sees a golden retriever puppy in a pet store. She feels bad seeing how small the dog's cage is and has heard how good goldens are with kids. Christmas is around the corner. . . . She buys the puppy and surprises her kids, who are over the moon. All sorts of promises and deals are made about feeding the dog, playing with the dog, brushing the dog's coat, and taking the dog out for walks. But after a few months, when the novelty of having a puppy wears off, and the dog continues peeing and pooping in the house because he was never properly trained or his humans don't take him out enough, and he keeps destroying shoes and remote controls because he hasn't been given enough exercise (and because that's what puppies do sometimes, even if they *have* been properly exercised), Susan is at her wit's end. None of her friends or colleagues want the dog; all she's done is complain about all the stuff he's ruined. Off he goes to a shelter. Just for being a puppy and for having the bad luck of being bought by a family who was ill prepared to handle the responsibility.

Of course, either one of these dogs could be the dream dog Mike and Maggie Malone have been wanting for years. They're finally settled into married life; their careers are going well; and they've even got a cute new house with a fenced-in yard. They're primed and ready for their new best friend. And either of these precious dogs, who just want to be loved and just want a family, would be the most loyal and faithful companion they could ever ask for. But both dogs get dumped at a shelter, then killed. And a new golden retriever gets created and sold to the Malones, instead.

Because so many people are still purchasing animals, people keep breeding them. Why do we buy dogs who were deliberately bred, as opposed to adopting dogs who will be killed? I think the main reason is accessibility and lack of knowledge. Most people don't know where their local shelter is, but they pass by a pet store every other day. The allure of those precious animals in pet stores is irresistible—if you've already decided you're going to get a dog and then you go inside a pet store "just to look," you're a goner. Even if you haven't decided to get a dog, you're a goner once inside a pet store. Pet stores just seem more accessible than shelters, and most people have no idea that so many adoptable animals are sitting in shelters waiting for them. But really, how much effort would it take for us to find our nearest shelter?

The other main factor keeping us from adopting is fear. And I think the fear factor is two-fold:

1) Fear of not getting what we want: "We want purebred Labrador retrievers; the shelter won't have those."

2) Fear of stepping foot inside a shelter. None of us wants to see just what goes on inside these places. None of us wants to feel the pain of what we'll witness. None of us wants those feelings and images and memories ingrained in our heads. So we continue to pretend we're not part of the problem, and that the problem doesn't even exist, and look at my brand new puppy I just bought, isn't he cute?

It's been said that fear is actually False Evidence Appearing Real. So here's the real evidence to eradicate the fear:

Fact: Purebreds get dumped at shelters, just like mixed breeds do. In fact, 25 percent of shelter dogs are purebreds.[2]

But don't overlook the mixed breeds—mutts are healthier than purebreds because they have fewer diseases and lower instances of breed-specific ailments. It's Biology 101: Genetic diversity means reduced likelihood of breed-specific health problems.

Fact: Yep, most shelters will probably leave us feeling sick and heartbroken, but there's the very likely possibility that we could leave with the most grateful, angelic, miraculous creature we'll ever encounter, and save him or her from certain death. And instead of sticking our heads in the sand about the problem, we and our new best friends will be a walking billboard for shelter adoption. Who knows how many dogs we can save just by telling others where our adoptee came from? Any time someone asks about Lucy, "What is she?" meaning, what breed, I answer, "100 percent shelter." I never let the opportunity pass to tell someone that such a cute little moppet came from the shelter and that the day she was pulled, 180 dogs were killed.

WHO, ME?

Considering that all the animals I've ever had have come from friends, I don't know why I was shocked to learn that the majority of our country's pets are obtained through friends, family members, or acquaintances.[3]

This blows my mind—it means that *we* are responsible for the over-population. I mean, no duh, but still. Every time we have a pet who we don't spay or neuter and he or she has a litter—assuming we don't dump them in a shelter—we need to find them homes. And all these homes could instead be adopting animals from shelters—animals like the millions of strays that Animal Control picks up every year.

Why aren't pet parents spaying and neutering their animals? Sometimes men equate neutering their dog with neutering their own manhood. Men: your dogs' nards aren't yours. You can still be a man if your dog has no nards. You can still be a man if *you* don't have nards. Nards do not make a man. Character does.

A lot of people love their dog's character so much they want to have another one just like him or her. Or they want to enjoy the process of having their dog birth a litter. The family who gave me Timber and Joey falls into this category. I think a lot of families do. They want their kids to experience the miracle of life, the whole process. I get it. So families allow or facilitate the dog to breed, they keep one or two pups from the litter, then find homes for all the others. And therein lies the problem. Timber and Joey came from a litter of twelve. So including the two breeders, that's up to fourteen homes that have just been used up that could've rescued dogs from death row. I love my dogs, of course, but had their parents been spayed and neutered, fourteen other dogs could've been spared.

SEX POLICE

....

Don't get me wrong: I'm not all excited about spaying and neutering. I hate to say it, but I think there's something arrogant about spaying and neutering animals. Like if aliens from outer space came down to Earth and started sterilizing us, because we've overpopulated our Earth. Or if our own parents got us sterilized as infants. Our doing it to animals is definitely messed up. But killing millions of dogs and cats every year while millions more languish in shelters and on the streets is more screwed up. Spaying and neutering is the lesser of two evils. This is the mess we've made of things and this is the reality we now need to deal with. So until we have a better solution to the horrific problem we created, I will spay and neuter my companion animals and encourage others to do the same.

It's also the humane thing to do for the individual animal. It makes them less aggressive and it makes other animals less aggressive toward them. It reduces the likelihood of uterine infections, breast cancer, and testicular cancer.[4] And it also keeps them from the agony of being in heat and not being able to do anything about it. Animals in heat will do almost anything—jump fences, crawl under fences, and break out of houses—anything to sex it up. So spaying and neutering also means less of a chance of losing your beloved.

(P.S. Unfixed animals spray stinky pee all over the place.)

LOSERS

....

We are so irresponsible, we shouldn't be allowed to have pets. Each year in the United States, 600,000 to 750,000 cats and dogs are reclaimed from shelters by their families.[5] That many people are losing their animals? (I shouldn't be so shocked. I was one of those people back in college.) Even more disheartening is that only 15 to 20 percent of dogs and less than 2 percent of cats are reunited with their human companions.[6] So clearly, the number of animals being lost is in the millions. Either people are lax about searching for their animals (maybe they're secretly glad they're gone), they don't know what to do so they don't contact the nearby shelters, or, hoping their animals will come home, they wait a few days before contacting the shelters.

Sometimes, this delay can be the difference between life and death. Different states have different statutes about how long a shelter must hold an animal before euthanizing him or her. Generally, animals are held about five or six days, although animals who are licensed typically have a slightly longer hold period.

(I'm laughing to myself, imagining if dog licenses were like driver's licenses and what Timber, Joey, and Lucy's license pictures would look like.)

CHAPTER 3

DON'T GET MAD, GET ADOPTING

A nytime there's a news story about a lone kitten trapped in a sewer or a single dog being swept away by a flood current, the world watches, transfixed and in prayer. But few of us pay mind to the millions in cages, or the thousands being killed every day.

I shove Timber and Joey behind a bush while I tell people about Lucy's adoption. I'm ashamed that they aren't rescues. When Reggie and I were feeling ready for dogs, I knew I didn't want to buy a dog from a breeder or pet store. I knew about the pet overpopulation problem and didn't want to be a part of it. I also thought it was creepy to buy an animal—you don't buy or sell a baby, why should you buy or sell any living being, like it's an object? So we spent the weekend going to adoption events at a few local Petcos. We both had our hearts set on Labs. We left each event feeling disappointed. As ridiculous as I now know it is, we thought we'd never find two Lab puppies. The very next day, I got a call at work from a friend. Her sister's dog had just given birth, and knowing what a big animal lover I was, she wanted me to hear the sounds of the mewing puppies over the phone. They sounded like kittens.

Me: "Reggie and I just spent the weekend looking for puppies. Labs."

Her: "These are Labs!"

Me: "Oh, well, we're going to adopt dogs because it's uncool to buy and sell animals."

Her: "She's not selling them. She's just looking for good homes!"

Me (excitement growing, forgetting all about the millions of animals being killed every year): "Well, we were planning on adopting *two* dogs because we want them to have each other while we're at work."

Her: "You can totally have two. There were twelve in the litter!"

The day after looking for Lab puppies and worrying there were none, now two were practically being dropped into my lap. I was powerless. And of course, I adore Timber and Joey. That said, I wouldn't do it again knowing what I know now. Newborn Lab pups born into a good home— my friend's sister could've easily placed them with anyone. But now, two shelter pups would die because someone like me who knew about adoption wouldn't show up to save them. (Yes, puppies also get euthanized, not just adult dogs. Not just sick ones. Not just ones who are "unadoptable.")

But truth be told, I'm not sure I was willing to go to a shelter back then. I think I was avoiding it. Going to an adoption day at a store where a rescue group brought dogs—that I was up for. I was terrified to go to a shelter. I did not want to see cage after cage, face after face, of sad, scared, death-sentenced dogs. Especially if I was going to be choosy and not leave with a single one. Or if I was going to leave with one or two, what about the others I left behind? I did not want that on my conscience. I believe most people are just too scared to walk into a shelter. I was. I still am. If and when the time comes to adopt another dog, he or she may drop in my lap like Lucy did. (One of the perks of being in the animal rights community is that you know so many rescuers, you never have to set foot in a shelter.) But if no dogs fall from the sky, I won't let that shelter-fear stop me. These dogs deserve better. Covering my eyes or pretending it's not happening won't make the problem go away.

Nowadays, with the Internet, if you really are unwilling to go to a shelter, you can at least adopt from a rescue group that gets animals from shelters. Or a group that gets animals from families before they dump them at a shelter. Either way, you get a best friend, and it's one less dead animal. Petfinder.com, AdoptaPet.com, and Foundanimals.org are great resources for people looking to adopt.

SHELTERS

I remember the first time I read about the pet overpopulation crisis. At first, I was furious at the shelters. Why couldn't they figure out how not to kill animals? For a short period of time, I thought about opening one, until further research revealed just how catastrophic the overpopulation problem is. So you're not alone if you're thinking, "The shelter system is horrible. They shouldn't be killing animals, they should be placing them in good homes, or providing them with a clean, happy place to live until they die naturally." There are some no-kill shelters that do just this, and they serve as great models for what's possible. Sadly, though, many no-kill shelters turn animals away for lack of space. So for now, euthanasia is a grim reality.

It's easy for us to be mad at the system and point fingers and shake fists. But if there are only a certain number of shelters in existence and each one can only accommodate a certain number of animals—and the number of animals who are dumped at shelters every day far, far, far exceeds what these shelters can accommodate—what's the alternative? Overcrowd animals into shelters, and let them languish in cramped cages and kennels with limited food, no human contact, love, exercise, or stimulation? Watch them turn on each other and maim or kill one another? Force them to suffer this existence for the duration of their lives? Yes, well-managed no-kill shelters with 100 percent adoption rates and lightning-fast turnover rates are the ideal, but sadly, there aren't enough of those yet to rehome the millions of animals who go through the shelter system every year.

MAN'S BEST GARBAGE

Today I got an email asking for petition signatures to protect homeless animals. As I went on Twitter to share the petition, I saw a tweet about and a picture of a fourteen-year-old border collie, with a look of betrayal, terror, confusion, and sadness. He was walking in circles. Fourteen years old, and he had been dumped at a shelter by his family. He will either die lonely and heartbroken in this cage, get euthanized, or be rescued by a human angel who loves, cherishes, and spoils him for the rest of his life.

I cannot imagine a single circumstance—not a single one—that would have me ditching one of my beloved animals at a shelter. This poor, innocent angel deserved more from his family. I know that during this terrible recession, a lot of people have lost their jobs and homes. Many have given up their dogs, feeling that they had no other option. But I also know that many people in the same dire circumstances chose not to abandon their dogs at shelters; they found alternatives. As would I. Leaving them at a shelter wouldn't cross my mind for a millisecond; it's just not an option. I would live in a tent, in a car, or on the street with my dogs or place them with someone who could care for them. Dumping them in a shelter and having them euthanized because I don't have a home or a job isn't even in the realm of possibility. When I adopted them, it was for life—even when they destroyed everything, even when it was inconvenient, even when I was going through tough times. And it will still be for life even when they become old and their bladders and bowels start failing, and even when vet bills start to mount. They are living beings. I assumed responsibility for their care, and I will see the commitment through until they pass on. If there ever comes a time when I am unable to do so, I will ensure that they are placed with someone who can. This doesn't make me a hero, a martyr, or an animal rights activist—it just makes me a dog mom.

Just thinking about leaving my dogs in a shelter is devastating and inconceivable. They'd be so confused, so stressed, and so sad. It's been eight days since I've given the two big kids back to Reggie and Gina, and I've only had one pang of missing them. After all these years of sharing them, I've gotten good at turning off the part of my heart that yearns for them. Instead, I have to relearn to pick up food I drop while I'm cooking. (When Timber's around, I never have to pick up anything. As the director of food services, he keeps the kitchen floor spotless.) For the first few days, I always worry that Reggie and Gina have forgotten the feeding protocol. This particular time, I successfully fight the urge to send an email outlining all the basic care instructions for them. I don't always beat this urge, and thankfully, Reggie and Gina are very kind and understanding and good at humoring my neurosis. I also, on occasion, start imagining that one of the dogs will be on their deathbed during this trip and I won't make it to Northern Cali in time to see him or her off. But beyond the minor passing obsessions, I do okay while they're gone—especially with Lucy lapping up the extra attention.

Today, Reggie sent me a picture and two videos of the dogs swimming in a lake. They were swimming back to shore, side by side, each holding the end of a shared stick in their mouth. Their tails were swishing side to side, like rudders or propellers, or happiness indicators. I wish I knew which. I love them so much. I'm so happy to see them so happy. But in an instant I go from happy to worried—that when they're with me, their lives aren't as fulfilling. Is this what's going on in the minds of the people who turn their dogs and cats in to the shelter? Do they feel like they're bad pet parents, like they aren't doing a good job, and that they should relinquish their animals? None of us can be perfect parents all the time. And the beauty of dogs is that they are the most forgiving, loving, adoring, worshipping animals on the planet. Even if you're a bad, boring, deadbeat, couch-potato parent, they still want you. Yes, for some people, the most generous thing they can do for their pets is acknowledge that they aren't cut out for this animal at this time and find him or her a better family.

My sister and I had a cockatiel named Snowflake when we were little. When we first got her, we were all up in her business. But as time wore on, we neglected her. My dad, a compassionate man and the primary source of my animal obsession, did right by Snowflake and found her a new home where she was actually wanted. Rehoming can often be better than a dead-beat parent. But an open admission shelter is never better than a deadbeat parent. If you're getting rid of the animal once and for all and you'll never have to care for him or her ever again, you just need to do this one last thing and then you'll be free of all responsibility and all guilt. There can be no other option. You have to rehome your pet.

With all my heart, I hope that the shelter system gets overhauled and a better system is implemented. But hoping doesn't help. We, each and every one of us, need to do better for the animals. And in this case, it means we need to *stop buying animals*. It's that simple. Whatever type of dog or cat we want, we can get them at a shelter or from a rescue group—or from someone who is no longer willing or able to keep his or hers. Like the border collie.

We all get that sick feeling seeing sad animals in tiny pet store cages. And we desperately want to rescue them by buying them and taking them out of there. But every time we do that, we perpetuate a vicious cycle. There are so many unbearable tragedies in the world. So many, that we feel overwhelmed and helpless. But this is one we can actually end.

CHAPTER 4

THE SEX TRADE

Based on the simple principle of supply and demand, if we stop buying dogs from pet stores, puppy mills will stop producing them. Puppy mills are large-scale breeding operations. Picture a dilapidated, ramshackle structure crammed with stacked cages, with little protection from the elements. Or sometimes no structure and just a collection of cages outside, with no protection from the sun, wind, rain, snow, heat, or cold. Then think of malnourished, sick, injured, wounded, inbred dogs, living in this squalor. Then think of the mill operator who keeps these dogs like this, waiting for them to have litter after litter of puppies, just so he or she can take these sickly puppies, and make money selling them to pet stores (usually through a broker or middleman). Imagine these poor female dogs, going through pregnancy, labor, and delivery over and over and over again. When their poor, worn out bodies can't bear anymore, they are often killed. They are not regarded as living, feeling beings; they are factories whose sole function is to make money for the mill operators.

None of these animals are treated as family members; they're treated as items to be sold. They aren't given toys, treats, social interaction, grooming, or walks. In most cases, they aren't even given veterinary treatment. They live in stacked wire cages, and their feet and legs are often injured as a result. And since they don't get walked, they live in feces and urine until some other money-minded person takes them from the mills and sells them to pet stores all over the country. And then unsuspecting consumers, who fall prey to the cuteness and innocence of these poor animals, pay exorbitant amounts of money to bring one home. Little do they know that the following conditions and illnesses are common to puppy-mill dogs:

> Epilepsy, heart disease, kidney disease, musculoskeletal disorders, (hip dysplasia, dislocated patellas, etc.), endocrine disorders (diabetes, hyperthyroidism), blood disorders, deafness, eye problems (cataracts, glaucoma, progressive retinal atrophy, etc.), respiratory disorders, parvovirus, distemper, upper respiratory infections, kennel cough, pneumonia, mange, fleas, ticks, intestinal parasites, heartworm, and chronic diarrhea.[7]

There are countless stories of heartbroken people who purchase dogs from pet stores, only to get them home and watch their health rapidly deteriorate. They then spend thousands on vet bills, desperately trying to keep them alive, but losing them anyway. What if we stopped buying dogs from pet stores? If every single one of us said "never again," and meant it and stuck with it? Pet stores would be stuck with dogs no one was buying. How many more times would they purchase puppies from these brokers if people weren't buying them? At some point soon after our boycott, pet stores would stop contributing to this cycle of horror. And if the mills had no one buying their dogs, they'd stop their operations. It's just that easy to make a difference and put an end to this disgusting practice once and for all.

If people wanted a pet, they'd have to go to a shelter or a breeder. Obviously, the shelter is the better choice since their animals are going to be killed. Why not rescue one?

But what about breeders? Without question, there are breeders who have genuine love and respect for their animals (and their breed), and treat them as well as or better than we treat our own companion animals. That said, I don't agree with selling living beings, like they're objects or could possibly even be "ours" to sell—especially when tens of thousands are being killed every single day. I also think it's creepy to broker sex deals between animals. (If you go online and read some breeder talk, you'll see the creep-factor for yourself. Like how "bitches are in heat" for three weeks to two months and need to be crated for that entire period to keep them from breeding. And how the "male got at her." Or how they "hooked up." Or when one is "skipping a heat with one of my girls.") I'm sorry, I just think it's strange and unnatural to habitually control the copulation of animals and to be that intimately involved with your dog's estrus cycle. But if people are hung up on buying dogs from a breeder and comfortable with contributing to the exploitation of animals in that way, *at the very least*, they need to make sure they're not being duped by some puppy mill broker or backyard breeder posing as a "reputable breeder." Because make no mistake: they *all* claim to be "reputable breeders."

For starters, no breeders who care about animals will sell their dogs to any Joe Schmoe who answers their ad. They want to meet the prospective parents and do a home-check to see where the dog will be living. They'll have you fill out paperwork to see what your pet parenting background is. You'll be required to sign a contract saying you won't use the dog for breeding, and that if—for any reason at any time (even ten years later)—you decide you can no longer keep the dog, you'll return him or her to the breeder. This keeps the dog from being rehomed to a family who may not be up to snuff or from being ditched at a shelter.

As part of *your* due diligence, you need to request access to their entire facility, even if it's their home. This allows you to see that all the animals are being well cared for and well treated, that the people seem aboveboard, and that there's no shady stuff going on. You also need to meet the mother dog and ask for references of people who have purchased dogs from them in the recent past. If these requests are met with resistance of any kind, those are red flags that shouldn't be ignored.

Ugh—I hate even saying that phrase "purchased dogs." It just feels so wrong to talk about money and living beings in the same sentence. Really, at the very least, you should visit your local shelter before deciding on a breeder. Come on—just go. On behalf of the millions of animals dying in shelters, I *Beg* you. It's better for the shelter animals who are going to be killed; it's better for you because mutts are healthier than purebreds; and it's better for your wallet because adoption fees are far less expensive than breeder prices. You can thank me later, via email, and include pictures of your new beloved fur child.

CHAPTER 5

WORST IN SHOW

So just what is it about purebred dogs that makes us all so nutso? I know for me, it's purely a looks thing. Yep, as much as I hate to admit it, there are certain dogs I just find irresistible in the looks department. My "type" tends to be big and beefy, like Labs or pit bulls—or, even bigger, like Great Danes. Now, having fallen in love with my little Lucy, who is the furthest thing from my type, I know that looks are meaningless. And I know that I could fall in love with any dog. That said, a hunky slab o' dog will always turn my head.

When I was a kid, I watched the Westminster Dog Show with relish. My dog-loving dad would alert me that it was on and then set me up in either the family room or my parents' bedroom to watch. I quickly picked out my favorite dogs and anxiously waited to see if the judges would agree. Twice we were in sync: an Afghan hound one year and a Newfoundland another. (I don't remember the years, but I remember distinctly feeling that the Old English sheepdog and bulldog were strong contenders, too; my dad agreed.) At first, I was nothing but mesmerized by all the different breeds of dogs, especially the ones I liked and wanted. But I soon noticed something else. A slight discomfort. The excitement and joy of seeing all these amazing, beautiful dogs became tinged with this nagging feeling that maybe these dogs weren't thrilled to be "participating." The judges were poking at and prodding them, examining their ears, teeth, tails, stances, and even their private parts. (I remember a dog snapping at a judge not once, but twice.) The handlers were leading them around by these short, tight leashes. Many of the dogs were panting and seemed nervous, uncomfortable, and scared. I was too young to grasp that not only did the dogs have to endure *that* show, but that they were also made to travel to and from many shows, sometimes even overseas. I *wasn't* too young to understand that these dogs were being made to perform for the pleasure of humans. I don't think I realized that I was one of those humans—I think I just blamed the owners and handlers and judges. But I knew that I felt bad for the dogs while I was watching, and eventually, I stopped.

A year or two later, my parents took my sister and me on a ski trip to Great Barrington, Massachusetts. They booked rooms at a woodsy bed-and-breakfast on a few pastoral acres. The biggest draw of the place, though—and why my parents chose this one over all the others they had brochures for—was that the proprietors had two collies living there. Our dog, Candy, had died a few years earlier, and we were all excited to have some live-in doggie love as part of our vacation. We got to the place and it was pretty and charming. We met the owners and they were nice and friendly. We were shown to our rooms and they were cute and cozy. *Blah, blah, blah—where were the dogs?*

"Oh, they're show dogs, so we have them in a kennel on the other side of the property."

Huh?

"Because they're show dogs, they can't run around and be wild and play like other dogs. They'd get dirty and matted. We have to keep them kenneled."

Um, can we see them?

The woman begrudgingly led us out of the house and on a few minutes' walk to the edge of the property. There were two gorgeous collies in this small, sparse, chain-link kennel. We could see from a distance that they were big and beautiful, with silky coats, and that they certainly looked like regal show dogs. But even yards away, their eyes and body language screamed that they were just regular dogs and that they desperately wanted love and attention.

They started barking in excitement as we approached. But it wasn't like anything my family had ever heard. It was scratchy and raspy and muffled-sounding.

What's wrong with their voices?

"Oh, we had them debarked."

What?

With a wave of her hand, the woman explained, "It's a surgery where they cut away part of their vocal chords." I could feel the heaviness of my whole family, heartbroken that these two sweet dogs, through no fault of their own, had wound up with cut vocal chords, living in a kennel. Of course they were barking a lot—they were imprisoned in a kennel, got no love or affection, and the only time attention was paid to them was when they were forced to behave like pageant puppets. It's like putting a baby in a woodshed, then being irritated he's crying for food, nurturing, or a diaper change. Devastating.

We squeezed into the kennel to give the dogs some love. We had picked this place so we could get love from dogs. But now, all we wanted to do was give, give, give to these poor dogs. I had the sense that the woman thought it was somewhat irritating and silly, like these were just show dogs, not love dogs.

I think the Westminster Dog Show is at best irritating and silly, but more than that, it does a disservice parading around these purebreds. It's a disconcerting pairing of beauty pageantry and eugenics. Think about it: a bunch of rich white men create this list of rules and desirable traits for each breed. Then a bunch of people obsessively set out to try and create these Frankendogs by involving themselves in their sex lives; then a bunch of other people become experts in "training" and "handling" these dogs for these ridiculous contests; and then an even bigger group of people (us) pays money to own these dogs and/or watch them get dragged around a sporting arena and have their testicles tugged on.

Bulldogs, who were bred deliberately to have large heads, now need to be delivered by C-section 80 percent of the time.[8] They have more instances of hip dysplasia than any other breed, are more likely to die from respiratory illness than any other breed, and are the second-most likely breed to die from congenital disease.[9] They have problems with their eyes, ears, skin, respiratory systems, immunity, and neurological systems. They seem to be worse off than all other breeds and, without question, are one of the—if not *the*—most expensive breeds to have due to vet bills.

Boxers are prone to epilepsy. Dogs with smushed-in faces have a higher likelihood of breathing and cooling problems (which can be fatal), dental and jaw issues, and eye problems. My friend's beloved Boston Terrier needed to have an eye removed—which is not uncommon. Breeds with bulging eyes sometimes have an eye "pop out."

King Charles Cavalier spaniels have been so overbred that their skulls can be too small for their brains, leading to neurological disorders. They're also afflicted with severe heart disease.[10] Sixty percent of Golden Retrievers in the United States die from cancer.[11] Labradors commonly suffer from hip dysplasia; Dachshunds have back problems; and corgis have bone and joint issues brought on by breeding for dwarfism. The list goes on and on.

Every breed has problems due to selective breeding or inbreeding. Every single one. And yet breeders keep cranking these dogs out, despite the suffering the dogs will endure, and the heartbreak and financial distress it will bring the families who love them. Whether they're financially motivated; passionate about trying to create the "perfect" dog with the "perfect" bloodline; or they just love the breed, breeders are playing God and doing a really lousy job.

With the likes of the American Kennel Club (AKC) and the Westminster Kennel Club (WKC) calling the shots, underdogs don't stand a chance. Before Reggie and I adopted Timber and Joey, we'd stop at this "kennel club" we used to drive past all the time. We knew we weren't buying, but we wanted to get our dog fix and to love on the poor beings who were kenneled and waiting to get out. Every dog had a little index card on his or her kennel with breed, date of birth, and gender. And every card also said the dogs were AKC. This always impresses people looking for dogs. But guess what? It doesn't mean anything. Anyone with thirty dollars can register their dog with the American Kennel Club. It doesn't necessarily mean the breeders know what they're doing, treat their dogs well, or produce healthy pups. Dogs who are blind, deaf, and have breed-inherent problems are all eligible for registration.

Two other horrors that breeders propagate are tail docking and ear cropping. I always thought Dobermans were born with those triangular, erect-looking ears and short, stubby tails. But no—when they're just a few days old, vets, at the request of breeders or parents, perform *cosmetic surgery* on these poor animals. All so the dogs look a certain way—the way that Westminster and the AKC think they should look. Candy, the dog I grew up with was a miniature schnauzer. When my parents got her from the breeder, her tail was docked and her ears were cropped. I asked my parents about it the other day; they were both horrified and said they'd never condone or support this today. Can you even imagine holding a newborn baby in your arms and deciding then and there that her nose should be different, and sending her in for rhinoplasty? It's insane. And incredibly cruel. It needs to be abolished.

The tail is an appendage, made up of muscle, nerves, blood vessels, and vertebrae. Chopping it off is sick. In the old days, it was thought that tail cropping could prevent rabies. It was also done because it was thought to reduce the likelihood of tail injury for working dogs and dogs used for baiting and fighting. Thanks to modern science, we now know that tail docking increases risk of urinary and fecal incontinence, painful perineal hernias, and problems with the anus and rectum—and that it's totally cruel. It's usually done without anesthesia. It also causes social problems for dogs, who use their tails to communicate with other animals and humans. In a situation that they might normally be wagging their tail, they now only have a small nub, hardly visible to other dogs who are approaching. So tail-docked dogs can be perceived as aggressive or threatening because they have no wagging tails clearly visible from a distance. Being constantly *perceived* as aggressive can actually *make* these dogs aggressive—which is probably the desired outcome for some thugs who not only want their dogs to look fierce, but act fierce, too. But the rest of us know that having well-socialized dogs makes life better and easier for us and them.

Ear cropping is as senseless and cruel as tail docking. You've probably seen schnauzers, boxers, Great Danes, Doberman pinschers, pit bulls, and Boston terriers who've been subjected to this trauma. Breeders, misinformed vets, and pet parents will claim it's beneficial for dogs who are inclined to have ear infections and that the floppy earflap is more likely to trap moisture inside the ears. But this is simply not true. Thankfully, many vets are in the know and refuse to do the procedure; many vet practices even take a formal stance opposing ear cropping. According to Dr. T. J. Dunn, "As a veterinarian with thirty-two years of experience . . . I cannot find medical justification for cropping a dog's pinnas (outer ear)." Not only is it medically unjustifiable, but also ear cropping doesn't always achieve the desired aesthetic results, either. As a new vet, Dr. Dunn worked at a very busy small animal hospital in an affluent Chicago suburb, where every day, purebred dogs were admitted for the surgery and postsurgical bandaging. He assisted with cleaning and treating the occasional infected incision, and with rebandaging pups that came back in because one or both ears weren't standing properly. He listened to disappointed humans ask the surgeon, "What went wrong with the surgery?" when the actual outcome didn't meet the desired outcome.[12]

Depending on where they practice, vets can charge anywhere from $150 to $900 per surgery. So it's certainly lucrative for them to believe that ear cropping is beneficial for the dogs. It's a vile practice that should be outlawed.

I just went online and read a post about how bad one dog parent feels for making her previously abused dog go through the surgery. But she "love[s] how the cropped ears look," so is going do it anyway. I think part of the problem is how checked out people are from the reality of the actual surgery. In usual cases, the dog is first given a calming sedative, then a brief IV anesthetic for placement of the breathing tube in the windpipe, and then the "gas mask" anesthesia during the surgery. Then comes the cutting. They start at the base of the ear and cut up the center, going all the way to the tip. This is done, according to PetMD.com, to "remove the outer half of the ear. . . . What remains is a triangular piece of ear." Removing *half the ear* so that what's left is a triangular *piece of ear*? How disgusting—it's like a Hannibal Lecter movie. Except it's real life; it's being done to puppies; and it's being done by the very people who should be loving and protecting them. When the ear carving is done, the incision is either sutured or glued. As if the sedative, two anesthetics, and mutilation weren't enough, these poor babies also have to endure the removal of sutures ten to fourteen days later, as well as specific bandaging to keep the ears erect, which could take six to eight weeks (with weekly vet visits).[13]

Imagine if your spouse—whom you adored and worshipped—loved you and liked how you looked, but favored a slightly different aesthetic. And one day, he or she conspired with some other people who had the same strange proclivities to put you under anesthesia and surgically alter you to better fit that preference. It's just that sick.

Thankfully, there are many vets opposed to ear cropping, tail docking, and debarking. You'd think they'd all be, right? Don't be afraid to ask your vet whether he/she does these procedures. And be sure to let him or her know that you find these practices unnecessary, irresponsible, and abhorrent.

CHAPTER 6

CATS ARE PEOPLE, TOO

L et's not forget our feline friends. If you're a cat parent, let your vet know you're opposed to declawing. When I was in college, I adopted Binger, the cutest black kitten. I had been kicked out of my dorm freshman year for a marijuana incident. *(Sorry, Mom and Dad.)* I wound up living off campus and quickly made the most of the situation by getting a kitten. I had had a dog, cats, and birds growing up, but he was the first animal I adopted on my own. I loved Binger madly, but couldn't wait to get him declawed. Every time I stood at the stove cooking, he'd pickax his way up to my shoulder using his claws. It killed. I felt bad and worried about the operation, but didn't do any research or question asking. It was just something I "knew": cats ruin your furniture, so you have to get them declawed.

When he came back from the surgery, obviously in pain, I felt horrible. Had I allowed simple common sense to pervade my teenage brain, I would've known that declawing a cat is cruel and barbaric. Mother Nature gave him claws, and I had them surgically removed so he wouldn't scratch me or my furniture? How selfish and stupid.

It's also incredibly dangerous: Three years after I got him, right when I was about to graduate from college and move back home to New Jersey, Binger got lost outside. I went out looking for him and calling his name every day, multiple times a day. I made signs and hung them around the neighborhood. Because he had no claws, he had no way to hunt for food or defend himself from other animals. I was beside myself, wrought with worry and guilt. I didn't know if he'd ever find his way back home, or if he'd starve to death or get attacked and killed.

It had been nine days since Binger went missing and I was despondent. A neighbor had asked if Binger knew the sound of my car. He did. (When my roommates came home, he wouldn't always wait at the door. When I came home, he would.) My neighbor suggested I drive around looking for him instead of walking. That day, I drove around calling his name out the window and whistling for him. That night, he came home. I heard meowing outside the door. I was stoned, so I didn't quite know if I had imagined it or if it was real. I opened the door, and there he was, visibly skinny. He was all sketched out and didn't seem to trust me or remember me completely. He had lost a lot of weight—he was only able to catch and eat flies. But he was alive, by the grace of God, and we recovered from the traumatic incident and moved past it. But having gone through it, I knew I'd never declaw a cat ever again. And in the fifteen plus years since then, I've also learned about the cruelty inherent in declawing. (I've also long since given up smoking pot, FYI.)

Declawing is no joke. It's not just cutting claws—it's an amputation of the toes at the last joint. Not only is the nail removed, but so is a portion of the *bone.* Long-term complications can result, including permanent lameness, arthritis, displaced bone fragments, abnormal posture and movement, and tissue displacement. In severe cases, cats are in so much pain they only move by walking on their "elbows."[14] And immediately after the surgery, it's not like they can stay off their feet. They have to walk to their food and water and climb in and out of their litter boxes.[15] All after having the bones of their toes partially amputated. It's devastating. And it's just so we can preserve our couch cushions? Vets can make between $100 and $450 per declaw. Any vet who is willing to maim cats is no vet I'd want around my animals.

In Australia, Brazil, Israel, and many European countries, cat declawing is not only frowned upon, it's against the law. And with the growing awareness of the cruelty involved, it's losing favor in the United States, too. Multiple cities have been passing laws to outlaw this barbaric practice.

About six months after I graduated from college, Binger and I were living at my parents' house in New Jersey, while I was commuting to my new job in New York City. The day before I left for a ten-day trip to Italy, he made this weird coughing noise that I had never heard before. It wasn't the typical hairball thing—it was something else. He was totally fine in every other way, but I felt a little worried leaving him. I left him in the care of my parents and their three cats, one of whom Binger was friends with and liked playing with.

I went to Italy, had a great time, and came back. My precious little Binger was waiting by the door when I got home. He seemed fine, as if that coughing thing had never happened. And my parents reported that he never coughed once while I was gone. We loved on each other all night, and he slept in bed with me, with his leg casually slung over my leg, like he always did.

The next afternoon, he started the weird coughing noise and tried to leave the room. My Aunt Marcia had recently said something about how when cats know the end is near, they go out alone into the wild. I had an instant sinking feeling that Binger was dying. In a panic, I followed him into the next room. The coughing got worse; he was also vomiting; and he again tried to get away from me. The whole thing happened so fast, probably in about sixty seconds. He seized up and made some kind of involuntary screeching cat sound, and that was it. His little black body was lying dead in front of me on the guest-room bed. My dad was standing in the doorway, aghast. When I was in high school, my mom had been a volunteer EMT for five years with our local ambulance corps and had taught me CPR when she had learned it. I immediately tried resuscitating Binger. I covered his muzzle with my mouth and breathed into his little body. When his chest rose, for a split second, I thought I'd brought him back to life. But I quickly realized his chest was rising with my breath, not his. He was dead. I was hysterical, and I think my dad was in shock. I don't know why, but we quickly got into the car and drove to the vet. I guess we just didn't know what else to do. I cried the whole way there, with his lifeless body in my arms. He was gone. He was really gone. When we described what had happened to the vet, he said it sounded like congenital heart failure; Binger had been born with a heart murmur.

We left his body there, and I cried the whole way home and for the whole rest of the night. I replayed his death over and over again. I regretted following him around from room to room when he was clearly trying to be alone. I wondered if I should've opened the door and let him go outside to die, even though he was an inside cat. And I agonized about how I'd never get another minute with him ever again. He was such an affectionate little monkey. When I held him, he'd wrap his arms around my neck, his legs around my waist, and he'd purr and drool in my hair. I'd never been so close to another animal, and the pain and grief were deep.

When I woke up in the morning, I was about to pick up where I had left off the night before, grieving and agonizing and replaying the last minute of his life. But I quickly made the decision not to. I had just started dating Reggie, and we had recently talked about what it had been like for him when his dad died. I got to see that there was another option available for handling loss. The only one I knew was to go totally insane. When I woke up that morning ready to lose my mind because my cat was gone, I opted out immediately. I chose instead to focus on the good memories. How he used to lie in my lap for the entire four-hour drive from Maryland to New Jersey, and back. And how if I stopped petting him, he'd bite my hand to remind me that I was his slave. How he used to be a hellcat and swat at my answering machine every time it clicked on and off. Or how late at night, at the witching hour, he'd do this wild scat cat dance around the house, and my roommates and I would go crazy laughing.

I affirmed that I had been a good mother. During college, when I'd sleep at my boyfriend's house, I'd bring Binger with me—even though my boyfriend was asthmatic. (I was a better mom than girlfriend.) Instead of beating myself up for following Binger from room to room those last moments, I basked in gratitude that I got to be there for him. And I got awestruck by the miracle that he waited for me to come home from Italy before dying—he coughed the day before I left, not once while I was gone, and then died the day after I got home. I decided that morning that I would not mourn Binger. And I never shed a single tear over him from that moment on. Until tonight, fifteen years later, while writing this.

I'm not sure if I'll have another cat. I'm so entrenched in dog-ville now it's hard to imagine having a cat. And for some reason, the idea of walking dogs and picking up their poop seems easier than scooping a litter box. How crazy is that? Ah, who am I kidding? I will totally have a cat again. I won't be able to resist the temptation of some poor, innocent feline who needs a home. And I'd feel bad having just one cat; I think it's nice for animals to live with their own kind. So I'll surely have at least two.

Sadly, the pet overpopulation issue is as bad for cats as it is for dogs. Worse, actually. Cats have a 10 percent higher likelihood of being euthanized (as opposed to being adopted) than dogs.[16] So if you're in the market for a kitty, rescue one. Shelters are overrun with beautiful, sweet, silly kitties who need loving homes. Even purebred cats wind up at shelters, just like purebred dogs do. So adopt one, or two, and become the indentured servant you were born to be.

Dear Reader,

I hope you've enjoyed the book so far. It's been kinda fun, despite the fact that we've got piles of dead cats and dogs everywhere, right?

I hate to say it, but the party's over. Well, maybe not over, but winding down a little. The grown-ups got back, and now we have to pretend to be more mature than we are. The next few chapters have a lot of adult information. So they'll require a little more concentration and effort. I've made it easy for you up until this point. But I'm afraid I can't hold your hand anymore. We'll be venturing beyond the realm of canines and felines, and heading into the real world. One with lions and whales and pigs and sharks. Sexy, right?

This expanded journey is a compelling, worthy, and noble one. I know you're up for it. But now would be a good time to stand up and stretch, take a bathroom break, get some food.

Oy, I just reread this—how boring does it seem like the next section is gonna be? It's not boring, I swear. It just has a lot of information, so you can't sail through it like you could the earlier chapters.

Blah, blah, blah. I'm bored with this letter.

Thanks for caring about animals and reading this book.

xoxo,
Rory

CHAPTER 7

BLINDED BY "SCIENCE"

DON'T HAVE A SEIZURE

G et this: In thirty-two states, unclaimed animals in shelters can be sold or given to laboratories (or to animal dealers who then sell them to laboratories), where they will be used for painful and deadly experiments.[17] This practice is referred to as *pound seizure*, and what it translates to is innocent dogs and cats being tortured in the name of science. Can you imagine the nightmare of losing your beloved best friend compounded by finding out that he or she has been sold to a research laboratory? Now, take yourself out of the equation and just imagine it happening to any individual animal. This isn't just a nightmare if it's our animals, whom we love—it's an atrocity for *any* animal to endure.

SICK, SICK, SICK

In 2009, a PETA (People for the Ethical Treatment of Animals) undercover investigation at the University of Utah revealed that dogs and cats—many described in their shelter notes as "friendly," a "good family dog," or one who "sits, shakes"—were being purchased each year from local shelters for as little as fifteen dollars for use in invasive and deadly experiments in which they had holes drilled into their skulls, medical devices implanted in their chests, and chemicals injected into their brains.[18] *Ahhhhhhhhhhhhhhhh!!!!!!!* (That's me screaming.)

Laboratories and Class B dealers (the middlemen who procure shelter animals for labs) specifically look for docile, friendly animals to experiment on. They want to be able to torture the animals without fear of being attacked. Because of their incredibly sweet and gentle natures, beagles are a favorite choice for experimenters—so much, in fact, that some commercial breeders breed them specifically to supply scientific institutions.[19]

Ah, the perfect victims.

I could open a bag of crazy right now about the people who do these things. But if we all agree to oppose animal testing and pound seizure, encourage our legislators to sponsor bills, and never dump our animals at shelters, we can move on.

Oh wait, sorry, I take it back. Before we skip off into the sunset, we need to address animal testing on a bigger scale. It isn't just dogs who get tested on, obviously. Guess how many animals are subjected to nightmarish experiments every year. Guess. Nearly 100 million in the United States[20] and likely 75 to 100 million more worldwide.[21] (Were you close?) Part of their misery is living in barren cages in labs and being psychologically traumatized, socially isolated, and deprived of everything normal and natural to them. That alone is bad enough. Worse: The only times they're taken from their cages are when they're being tortured. What gets done to them—all in the name of science—is out of a horror movie: forced to inhale toxic fumes, infected with diseases they'd normally never have, tumors grown on them as large as their own bodies, immobilized in restraint devices for hours, holes drilled into their skulls, skin burned off, spinal cords crushed, blinded, poisoned, shocked, force-fed chemicals, made to suffer seizures, starved, drowned, brain-damaged, addicted to drugs, surgically operated on repeatedly, wires and electrodes implanted in their brains, and on and on and on.[22] [23] [24] And of course, painkillers aren't legally required.[25] When experimenters are done with these poor souls—if they're still alive—they mostly kill them by gassing them, but also sometimes by breaking their necks or cutting their heads off.[26]

So we're clear, some of this occurs just so we can buy floor wax, lipstick, shampoo, and other totally stupid stuff. Some companies take a strong stand against animal testing; others put the almighty dollar first. (Manufacturing giant Procter & Gamble still tests on animals, despite constant pressure from animal rights organizations all over the world.) Even though product ingredients have been around for decades and have already been tested and even though alternative testing methods exist that don't include the use of animals, outdated animal testing is still rampant.

BETTY FORD CLINIC FOR ANIMALS?

No experiment, no matter how agonizing or absurd, is prohibited. For example, even though we've known for fifty years how dangerous smoking is, on behalf of some tobacco companies, scientists are stuffing animals into tubes and forcing them to inhale cigarette smoke for up to six straight hours a day, every day, for up to three years.[27] Phillip Morris International's website says: "The majority of our research using laboratory animals is focused on obtaining information to better understand the mechanisms by which tobacco-related diseases develop."[28] Um, tobacco-related diseases develop from using tobacco. I think we're all pretty clear on that by now.

Not only are they forced to inhale cigarette smoke, animals are also forced to ingest alcohol and drugs to the level of addiction.[29] A friend of mine is constantly battling nicotine addiction; another struggles with drugs and alcohol. They don't wish this agony on their worst enemies, let alone innocent animals.

WHERE'S THE CURE?

You'd think that with all this savagery inflicted on billions of animals, all the medical advancements and modern technology, and all the years animal testing has been going on, we'd have cured all human illnesses by now, right? So what's the deal? Why haven't we? You don't need a doctorate to understand: 1) the anatomy and physiology of nonhuman animals is different than ours; 2) diseases that are artificially induced in animals in a laboratory are never identical to those that occur naturally in human beings; 3) animals and humans metabolize drugs differently; and 4) the use of genetically modified animals and stresses of lab life create additional variables.[30] Nine out of ten experimental drugs fail in clinical studies because scientists can't accurately predict how humans will respond to them based on laboratory and animal studies.[31] Former director of the National Cancer Institute, Dr. Richard Klausner, said, "We have cured mice of cancer for decades, and it simply didn't work in humans."[32]

And in three decades of HIV/AIDS research, there have been more than eighty-five successful vaccines developed for primates, but as of 2012, zero out of more than 200 preventive and therapeutic vaccine trials have demonstrated significant benefit to humans.[33] Great—we've figured out how to infect mice with cancer and vaccinate primates.

It isn't just cancer and AIDS research, obviously, where animal testing can lead to disastrous results. In 2006, an immunotherapy antibody tested successfully on mice, rats, rabbits, and two species of monkeys.[34] But it nearly killed all the human subjects in its first stage of human testing, causing them permanent organ damage and creating future risk of cancers.[35] The human reaction to the antibody was the opposite of that seen in monkeys, who were given doses up to 500 times higher than those given to the human subjects![36] [37]

A few more:

- An estimated 140,000 people were killed by an anti-inflammatory that tested "safe" in at least eight studies in monkeys and five other animal species.[38] [39]

- A 2004 report documented nearly 200 treatments that prevented or delayed diabetes in mice, without any translation to human benefit.[40]

- Despite seeing benefits in animal studies for spinal cord injuries, there were no benefits in any of the twenty-plus human trials.[41]

- Similarly, every one of more than 150 successful stroke treatments for animals failed to improve survival in humans.[42]

The list of failed animal-tested treatments goes on and on, but I'm bored (and depressed). So I'll just leave you with this: one of the earlier, more publicized failures of animal testing was in the 1950s, when thalidomide was given to pregnant women to combat morning sickness. Over 10,000 babies were born with major birth defects; many died. Somehow, this spurred governments to mandate animal testing as a way to assure drug safety and perhaps assuage public concern. Ironically, thalidomide would still be approved today because none of the usual animal species used for birth-defect testing would show the abnormalities caused in humans.[43]

THE TRUTH AND LIES ABOUT VIVISECTION

According to John J. Pippin, MD, FACC, director of academic affairs for the Physicians Committee for Responsible Medicine (PCRM), "Unknown to most of the public, entire fields of medical discovery have produced little or nothing of value to humans from decades of animal experimentation."[44] And yet in 1994, without supporting citation, the U.S. Public Health Service erroneously reported animal research as being responsible for every major medical advancement in the last century.[45] And like all good untruths, it's been repeated countless times since then, despite being totally unfounded and completely untrue. Thankfully, a 2008 review by Robert Matthews published in the *Journal of the Royal Society of Medicine*[46] brought this humongous gaffe to light, but it may take time for it to permeate the scientific community. In the meantime, we the people need to stop repeating it and believing it. So let's start our nuero-reprograming now by repeating Dr. Pippin's assertion: "entire fields of medical discovery have produced little or nothing of value to humans from decades of animal experimentation."

The good news: There are countless scientists working with nonanimal research methods, including computational science, bioinformatics, systems biology, in-vitro techniques, tissue engineering, microfluidics, stem cells, human tissue studies, genetics, and microdosing.[47] Science is miraculous, and there's so much we still don't know. How many more decades need to go by, how many more billions of animals need to be tortured, and how many hundreds of millions more humans need to die before we make these alternatives the main focus of our research efforts?

It's been said that the definition of insanity is doing the same thing over and over again but expecting different results.

Not to worry, at this very moment, millions of dollars are being spent torturing animals to find a cure for insanity. (Oh yeah, and they're using our tax dollars to do it, through grants from the National Institutes of Health.)[48]

CHAPTER 8

THAT'S ENTERTAINMENT

ACT I

All my favorite movies and TV shows when I was a kid were ones about or featuring animals. Of course, there were the classics, like *Tom and Jerry*, *101 Dalmatians*, and *Scooby-Doo*. And I was wild about the Clint Eastwood films with his orangutan sidekick, Clyde. I desperately wanted some type of monkey or chimp, and for years, I asked my parents to get me one for my birthday. (Cue Veruca Salt from *Willy Wonka and the Chocolate Factory*: "I want the world. . . . I want the whole world. . . .")

Of course, it's that same love for animals that makes us want to see them on the big screen at every turn. They're cute and funny and silly, and just the same way we fantasize about our lives with some Hollywood actor, we fantasize about our lives with some Hollywood animal. The problem with all fantasies is reality. Thanks to the courage of undercover investigators who go into factory farms, we've all seen horrific farm animal abuse caught on tape. But there's a ton of animal cruelty in everyday stuff that hardly gets our attention, hiding in plain sight: print ads, commercials, TV shows, and movies. With good editing, all we see are happy-looking animals.

Those chimps we see "smiling" in ads and films and on TV—those aren't smiles; they're fear grimaces. Studies of chimps in the wild confirm that they don't smile like humans do when they're happy; they only "smile" when they're afraid. They're taught to "smile" on command with fear-based training methods. They're physically and psychologically abused by trainers, causing them constant anxiety and fear, anticipating the trainer's every move.[49]

EVERY WHICH WAY BUT KIND

Did you ever wonder what happened to the orangutan Clyde, Clint Eastwood's sidekick in *Every Which Way But Loose*? Well, for starters, he was trained with a can of mace and a pipe.[50] To ensure his compliance, the day before filming started he was viciously beaten.[51] Toward the end of filming for the sequel, he got caught "stealing" doughnuts on the set.[52] So he was taken back to the training facility and beaten for twenty minutes with a three-and-a-half-foot axe handle.[53] He died a short time later from a cerebral hemorrhage.[54]

How many of those "silly, happy chimps" we've been laughing at all our lives are actually terrified because they've been terrorized? Primatologist Sarah Baeckler spent more than a year volunteering with a prominent

Hollywood animal trainer at a leading facility. Afterward, she—along with the Animal Legal Defense Fund—filed a lawsuit. She claimed that, "The trainers physically abuse the chimpanzees for various reasons, but often for no reason at all. If the chimpanzees try to run away from a trainer, they are beaten. If they bite someone, they are beaten. If they don't pay attention, they are beaten. Sometimes they are beaten without any provocation or for things that are completely out of their control."[55] In the past, the trainer had been fined, cited, and placed on probation for animal-related offenses, including failure to provide minimum space for chimps in a transportation vehicle, illegal possession of a lion cub, failure to provide ventilation in a shipping container for a chimpanzee, and failure to have an environmental enhancement plan.[56] And yet we've seen "his" chimps in many movies, commercials, and TV shows.[57]

Baeckler said she saw him kick and punch young chimps with all his strength.[58] And that he instructed her to hit the chimps "hard enough that they know you mean business, but not so hard that you do permanent damage."[59] "Kick her in the face as hard as you can. You can't hurt her."[60] He was sued over the alleged abuse and denied the claims. But as part of the settlement, he agreed to retire the chimps in his possession to sanctuaries and to not work with other chimps and certain other primates in the future.[61] (But he still works with other animals.)[62]

BEHIND BARS

Chimps have a short shelf life for performing, so trainers try to get them young, which means tricking, sedating, or forcibly restraining moms while tearing away their infants.[63] All chimps are typically retired before they turn eight, because at that age, they're too strong to be considered "safe" to be around humans.[64] They can live up to sixty years,[65] so "retirement" can mean fifty years of hell. When their fifteen minutes of fame are over and they're no longer wanted by their trainers, many chimps spend decades waiting to die in barren concrete cells at roadside zoos or pseudosanctuaries. During one investigation, a chimp who had been used in the 2001 production of *Planet of the Apes* was found living amid garbage, maggots, and excrement[66] in a dungeon-like underground cement pit[67] at a Texas roadside attraction.[68] Thanks for the memories.

I find it challenging just being a good dog mom. Seriously, it's hard work making sure my little three-pack are all well fed, exercised, mentally stimulated, and happy. It's incredibly arrogant, naive, and dishonest to think we can properly care for captive wild animals. Wolves, bears, big cats, and elephants all require expansive space to roam, explore, and hunt or forage. Most animals used in entertainment are confined to small enclosures or cages, causing major physical and psychological problems. The only time they're "free" is when they're being trained (with abusive methods), or when they're being forced to perform.

SOME ANIMALS WERE HARMED IN THE MAKING OF THIS FILM

You've likely seen movies using animals, and at the end of the movie, in the credits, seen something written like, "no animals were harmed in the making of this film" or "the use of animals in the film was monitored by American Humane Association (AHA)." AHA (not to be confused with the Humane

Society of the United States) is funded by the Screen Actor's Guild, so despite their best intentions, their policing isn't truly independent.[69] AHA is only there to monitor what happens *on the set*. They don't dictate how the animals are acquired, trained, fed, housed, treated, or disposed of when they're no longer able to "perform."

LIGHTS, CAMERA, ABUSE!

When I drove cross-country with Timber and Joey, when I was moving from New Jersey to California (October 2004), we stopped at this beautiful lake somewhere in Wyoming. I was euphoric about the move, loving the cross-country adventure, and blown away by the natural beauty of what was before me. I desperately wanted to take a picture of the dogs in front of the lake; I wanted it to be the dog version of a school picture. Timber and Joey had a whole other agenda, though. Trying to get each of them to sit still and look at the camera for just a few seconds was a nightmare. My human desire for a specific outcome had a head-on collision with their will to be dogs and do dog things. The result was me getting frustrated and yelling at them in a total "Mommy Dearest" meltdown moment. Every time I look at their school pictures from that year, I remember how willful I was, and how out of touch I was with their wants and needs. And these are my children, whom I love with all my heart. I can see how trainers could so easily view animals as hired help and how easy it would be for them to lose their tempers if they weren't getting the desired results. But it doesn't make it okay.

We watch a twenty-second TV spot or a two-hour tale woven together with magic and fairy dust, but we don't consider the logistics of the living beings involved. Any time animals are being used for financial gain, there's always potential for them to be mistreated, neglected, or abused.

THE ROAD TO HELL IS PAVED WITH DEAD PUPPIES

One of the problems inherent in using hired puppies in show biz is that they can be taken from their moms when they're too young. This can have major health implications for the pups and can even be fatal. Even if a production company and casting director have good intentions, bad things can happen. A few years ago, Disney made a film called *Snow Buddies*. Some of the movie's "stars" were golden retrievers, so dozens of puppies were imported from New York to Vancouver. Despite the USDA's Animal Welfare Act, the Canadian Food Inspection Agency's import regulations, and the guidelines listed by AHA, it's believed that twenty-five puppies were taken from their moms when they were just six and a half weeks old.[70] These babies traveled 3,000 miles by plane and then more by car, spending over twelve hours in transit—in cold weather.[71]

Unsurprisingly, many puppies were sick and had to be removed from the set. Some were euthanized. AHA rated the film as "Monitored: Unacceptable." But that label did not appear in the film's credits. AHA "only issues language for films with ratings of Monitored: Outstanding, Monitored: Acceptable, and Monitored: Special Circumstances."[72] Well, that's convenient . . . for everyone except the animals. If I weren't so busy being snide, I'd be furious.

CHIMPS AND PUPPIES AND HORSES, OH MY!

In 2005, during the filming of the 20th Century Fox film *Flicka*, one horse died and one was put down. One fractured a tibia and was euthanized, the other tripped on a lead rope, fell, and broke his or her neck.[73] AHA was there.

Between 2010 and 2012, three horses died on the set of the HBO series *Luck.*[74] AHA was there.

In 2012, it was reported that that twenty-seven animals died during production of the *The Hobbit*. AHA was there. The filmmakers "completely rejected the allegation." Their comments were all adamant that "No animals died or were harmed **on set during filming**" [the emphasis is mine], that they used computer-generated animals for more than 55 percent of the film, and that they were careful not use to animals in scenes that would be dangerous or stressful to them.[75] Great. But animals still died off set. Since "hundreds of thousands of dollars were spent on upgrading housing and stable facilities" it's clear the filmmakers' intentions were good. And yet there were still dead animals. AHA admits that they don't have the jurisdiction or funds to monitor the animals before production, off set during production, during the training period, or after the animals are retired. So AHA is asking for more funding and jurisdiction.[76] With all due respect: It's like trying to keep slavery legalized, but having someone get paid to oversee the slaves' proper treatment. Rather than asking for more money and power, I think this is the perfect time to call upon the film industry to stop using animals altogether. How about using that funding instead to hire more CGI (computer-generated imagery) experts so that all of the animals in films are computer-generated? What would the studios say to that? *Too radical?* I'd say the confinement, abuse, and untimely deaths of animals in film productions is a much crazier notion. *Too expensive?* The film industry grosses billions of dollars a year.[77] *Billions.* They can afford to stop hurting animals.

And we can live without movies that use real animals. If movie studios and TV networks spend a lot of money creating work that no one sees because we're protesting the use of live animals, they'll quickly change their ways. But as long as we keep taking our kids to dog, horse, and monkey movies, studios will keep making them.

ACT II

CIRCUSES: THE CRUELEST SHOWS ON EARTH

Obviously, when we have children, we want to do everything in our power to make them happy. Taking your kids to the circus is as much a part of parenthood as teaching them how to ride a bike. But sometimes we can be blinded to the bigger picture. We overlook the fact that the fleeting pleasure of our children causes a lifetime of suffering for animals.

Baby elephants don't grow on trees; they have loving, devoted, nurturing mothers just like we do—so devoted, in fact, that elephant mothers nurse their young for five years. Boy elephants remain with their mothers until adolescence, while daughters stay with their moms their entire lives![78] But, time and time again, these bonds are brutally broken so that we can watch elephants stand on their heads and balance on balls under the big top. In Asia and Africa, baby elephants around eighteen to twenty-four months who are still nursing are lassoed around their legs, pulled to the ground, and dragged away from their mothers.[79] Because the mothers are fiercely protective of their beloved children, they are often killed by the same poachers who kidnap and sell their calves.[80] Eyewitnesses have reported seeing baby elephants refusing to abandon their dead mothers, and even attempting to nurse from their corpses.[81]

Many circus elephants are born in captivity. Actress and animal activist Kathy Najimy narrated an undercover video of a captive birth at Ringling Bros. and Barnum & Bailey Circus. The laboring mom is standing on a cement floor, with one front leg and one hind leg chained. A laboring mother, chained by the legs! *(My blood is boiling.)* She can barely move. And unlike her wild counterparts, instead of having the usual herd of female elephants to support her during delivery, this mom has a handler standing next to her head with a bullhook—a "training" device which looks like a fireplace poker. *(My stomach is in knots.)* When the baby comes out, he falls between her two back feet—one of which is chained—onto the hard cement floor. *(Whose genius idea was that?)* She either steps on her seconds-old baby or nearly does—it's hard to tell from the video. Because of the chains, she can't see what's happening, and she kicks her newborn!

The audacity of these humans and this circus to think they need to manage this mother's delivery is sickening. Even a fool can see the mother and child would be better off left alone on a patch of grass, letting Mother

Nature run her course. But even after the birth, the audacity continues. The workers drag the newborn aside, leaving the mother chained, bellowing for her baby. The workers' attention is on cleaning the floor beneath her, not allowing mother and baby access to each other. The story doesn't have a happy ending, either. Eight months later, the baby boy fell from a circus pedestal during a training exercise and severely fractured both hind legs. So they killed him.[82] *This is "The Greatest Show on Earth"?*

Google "Ringling bound babies" to see what life is like for baby elephants "lucky" enough to survive. Sadly, once they're grown up, things aren't any better. Just like animals used in TV and film, animals "trained" for the circus are horribly abused. They're whipped, shocked, and beaten with bullhooks.[83]

Animal abuse happens at big, famous circuses and at smaller, unknown ones. And the misery and assault aren't just inflicted on elephants. It all happens to other animals, too, like horses, bears, lions, tigers, dogs, and any other animal you'd see at a circus. There are pages and pages documenting USDA citations, warnings, and complaints against circuses of all kinds. Everything you can imagine (and more), like failure to provide: adequate veterinary care; suitable housing; enough headroom (for caged animals); clean water; healthy food; appropriate socialization; environmental enrichment plans; protection from the elements; and sufficient ventilation. If that's not enough, there are also endless citations for excessive buildup up and improper disposal of manure; failure to maintain facilities to keep animals from escape or harming themselves; noncompliance issues for inspections; allowing animals access to hazardous materials; failure to handle animals in a manner that prevents trauma and harm; and failure to store food supplies in a manner adequate to protect them from deterioration, mold, or contamination by vermin.[84] These poor creatures can't even get a decent meal.

You'd think that these circuses with all these violations and citations would be in big trouble, right? Not so much. They receive a slap on the wrist and small fines. Sometimes, the USDA will take away a circus' animal license, which sounds like it would put the circus out of business. But nope, in these cases, they simply "lease" animals from some other crappy circus just like theirs.[85] *Lease*, like they're cars, and not living beings. There are no real consequences for wrongdoings. So why would circuses do right by the animals? They don't. (When Timber steals food and Lucy poops in the house, there are no real consequences, either. So why would they do right by me? They don't.)

When they're not being beaten into submission, circus animals are simply imprisoned in traveling jail cells. For example, the "prestigious" Ringling Bros. and Barnum & Bailey Circus spends eleven months a year touring the country, its three units traveling over 25,000 miles.[86] This means that elephants are sometimes chained for up to 100 hours at a time, and lions and tigers are forced to live and travel crammed into cages so small that they can barely turn around.[87] Animals can die of heatstroke in poorly ventilated boxcars or injure themselves while trying to escape the fatal heat.[88] So basically, their lives are completely wretched and miserable. But the show must go on—animals must be tortured, children must be entertained!

ZOOS

I'm supposed to write something nice first to butter you up, like how I loved going to the zoo as a kid. But it's just not true. I only went a handful of times. And as much as I liked seeing animals, it was obvious they were sad and suffering. Animals in the wild have complex, layered lives. They form close bonds with other animals; they have their own versions of families; they hunt or forage for their foods; they live near certain species and avoid living near others; and they can roam or migrate thousands of miles. The world is their oyster; they can come and go as they please, choosing where to eat, drink, bathe, sleep, hibernate, play, mate, fight, live, and die. No matter how hard they try, zoos cannot replicate the natural environments of animals. So why do they try? Why do they even exist?

Supposedly, zoos exist for research, education, and to help with endangered species, right? Let's start with research. The research of most zoos focuses on breeding animals in captivity and on how to keep them alive.[89] So this research really only serves the business of zoos. If there were no more zoos, we wouldn't need to know how to breed animals for zoos. Alas, some of these zoos and "natural wildlife safaris" have gotten so good at this "research" that many have an excess of animals being quietly peddled out the back door. Yep, these animals are either discarded or sold to brokers, private collectors, dealers, wholesalers, auctions, biomedical researchers, hunting ranches, and slaughterhouses for the exotic meat trade,[90] or for their hides.[91] Some zoos don't even have the good sense to be ashamed about this. One zoo's chief of veterinary services actually called on members of the zoo community to support the use of surplus zoo animals in medical experimentation![92] *Can you even?!* Among all the zoos in the United States, not a single one has a policy to provide lifetime care for the animals born there.[93] In fact, many zoos know in advance that they'll have a hard time placing the offspring of the species they're breeding—especially the males—once they mature.[94] But they breed them anyway, because babies are good for business.

But wait, aren't all zoos trying to help repopulate endangered species? A report by the World Society for the Protection of Animals revealed that only about 10 percent of the world's zoos are registered for captive breeding and wildlife preservation and that only 2 percent of the world's threatened or endangered species are registered in breeding programs.[95] Most animals in zoos are the popular ones that will draw a crowd, not endangered ones who are being prepared for reentry in the wild.[96] And according to George Schaller—one of the founding fathers of wildlife conservation—shuttling giant pandas around from one zoo to another for display is contributing to their near extinction; in-breeding is an issue with animals in captivity.[97]

In zoos, birds' wings are clipped so they can't fly; marine animals are crammed into tiny pools; and animals who normally live in groups are kept alone or in pairs. Natural hunting instincts are disregarded and stifled by regulated feeding, and their mating desires are ignored in favor of breeding programs. Understandably, all this causes abnormal and self-destructive behavior, called *zoochosis*.[98]

Anyone who's been to the zoo has likely left with a sick feeling, having witnessed animals displaying symptoms of boredom, loneliness, depression, anxiety, and neurosis. None of these behaviors are present in animals in the wild—they are unique to animals in captivity.

Zoochosis can present as bar biting; the continual licking of walls, bars, or gates in an enclosure; pacing; circling; neck twisting; repeated vomiting and the eating of vomit; playing with and eating excrement and smearing it on the walls and glass; rocking; swaying; head bobbing and weaving; obsessive grooming (pulling out feathers or hair, leaving bald spots); and self-mutilation (which includes biting or chewing the hands, feet, limbs, or tails, or hitting the head against a wall).[99]

A sanctuary that provides refuge for rescued zoo animals reported that the hands of the arriving chimps were "unrecognizable from all the scar tissue."[100] Public complaints about these tragic behaviors are so rampant, that some zoos administer drugs like Prozac to their animals.[101] *Stop the insanity!*

And if contending with their own insanity isn't enough, animals also have to endure human error, neglect, carelessness, and thoughtlessness. Many animals have died after ingesting coins, bags, and other stuff thrown into their enclosures during regular business hours.[102] One giraffe who died was found to have forty-four pounds of plastic in his stomach![103] Sadly, there's an endless litany of horror:

A bear starved to death at the Toledo Zoo after zoo officials locked her up to hibernate without food or water—not knowing that her species doesn't hibernate. At the Niabi Zoo in Illinois, a three-month-old lion cub was euthanized after his spinal cord was crushed by a falling exhibit door. Despite knowing that two Asiatic bears had fought dozens of times, the Denver Zoo continued to house them together until one finally killed the other. A kangaroo who was struck by a train running through the exhibit at the Cleveland Zoo was so severely injured that she had to be euthanized; she was at least the fifth animal to be struck by the train. A hyena at the Buffalo Zoo was crushed to death by a boulder in the exhibit. At the Saint Louis Zoo, a polar bear died during exploratory surgery, which revealed that pieces of cloth and a plastic trash bag had obstructed his digestive tract.

At the National Zoo, dozens of animals have died in recent years, including two zebras who died of malnutrition, two red pandas who died from eating rat poison that was spread in their enclosure, and an orangutan who was euthanized because zoo officials mistakenly believed that she had cancer.[104]

(By the way, the National Zoo isn't even a registered zoo—it's part of the Smithsonian museum. And this is in our nation's capital, one of the most popular and public zoos in America. If they're getting things so dismally wrong, what does that say about the rest of our country's zoos?)

By their very design, zoos leave animals vulnerable to natural disasters. In the event of floods, wildfires, or hurricanes, they're often abandoned to fend for themselves—except they can't, because they're in locked cages, pools, or enclosures. Some have starved to death, others burned alive in their cages.[105] Officials admitted they had no evacuation plan for the animals when there were wildfires raging near the Los Angeles Zoo.[106] During Hurricane Katrina, nearly 6,000 marine animals died at a New Orleans aquarium when the power failed and employees were forced to evacuate.[107] In the wild, animals at least have a fighting chance—they can seek out higher ground during flooding, or try and outrun or outfly wildfires. They often instinctually know when hurricanes and other natural disasters are imminent; wild animals can find refuge in time to save themselves.

Wild animals can also try and steer clear of dangerous people, but zoo animals are susceptible to human violence. When an elephant was transferred from the famous San Diego Zoo to the San Diego Wild Animal Park, she was chained, pulled to the ground, and beaten with axe handles for two days. A witness likened the blows to "home run swings."[108] When talking about elephants, a San Francisco zookeeper said, "You have to motivate them, and the way you do that is by beating the hell out of them."[109] Zoo animals have been beaten, bludgeoned, and stolen.[110]

So what about the educational component of zoos? Yes, there are little signs hanging up with basic info about the species and where they come from, but kids barely look at these signs. Many of them can't read anyway, and they probably aren't listening to their parents reading when there are monkeys smearing poo on each other and the ice-cream man just walked by. What will they actually learn at the zoo? Yes, of course, children will like getting to see animals up close. But what's so important for kids to learn that it could justify the imprisonment of one animal, let alone all of them?

I understand that we are biologically programmed to want to make our kids happy at all costs. It's what makes good parents good parents. I know it's a lot to ask that parents overcome this programming in any regard. But I'm asking, parents. I'm asking.

If you polled 1,000 parents asking what they want for their kids, 999 of them would say, "I just want them to be happy." The one who wouldn't say that is my friend, Tracy. She's not some psycho mom who doesn't care about her kids' happiness. She's actually one of the most amazing, loving, fun, kind-hearted, patient, brilliant moms I've ever seen. Of course she wants her children to be happy, but she wants one thing more than that. I was visiting her when her daughter Sydney was about eighteen months old. I kept commenting on how patient and polite Tracy was with Sydney. Her response was, "I just want her to be *nice*." Tracy is one of the happiest people I know; she's a winner at the game of life. So maybe for her, it's a given that her kids (she now has a second daughter, Ashley) will be happy. But Tracy's greatest quality is her kindness, and it's what she most wants to cultivate in her daughters. More than she wants *happy* kids, she wants *nice* kids who are kind to others.

One of the earliest lessons parents teach kids is to be nice to the doggie or soft with the kitty. Even though babies get excited and roughly grab at our family pets, don't we protect our pets and teach our kids to be gentle? Isn't it our job as parents to continue teaching kids kindness to animals, even if it means skipping the circus or zoo? I've met countless children who boycott both. They are proud of their decision; they want nothing to do with either; and they want others to follow suit. These kids are happy *and* kind. They're not scarred by knowing the truth—they're empowered by it.

And sorry, I don't mean to be the Grinch Who Stole Animals, but how is it reasonable to cram a bunch of fish and marine animals into a glass box, when they're used to having the whole ocean as their home? Aquariums are no match for the wild. Ditto for "swim with the dolphins" programs. Whales and dolphins can travel up to 100 miles in a day. In captivity, they live in a space equivalent to a bathtub, in gross, chemically treated water. It's no wonder captive marine animals die decades earlier than their wild counterparts.

Whales and dolphins are kidnapped from their beautiful homes, taken away from their families, and literally made to jump through hoops. Surely, God did not create these intelligent, sensitive, majestic creatures to perform trite tricks for humans.

RODEOS

I wish rodeos were outlawed. Calf roping, steer wrestling, steer roping, barrel racing, bull riding, bronco riding, wild horse racing, chuck wagon racing, steer tailing, horse tripping—it's like a sadist's list of "how many ways can we injure animals?" For those of you who don't know what calf roping is: A baby cow no more than three to four months old is released from a chute.[111] She runs, terrified, and a psychopath on horseback chases her down. He ropes her, whiles she's running at full-speed, which sends her flying in the air and off her feet (knocking the wind out of her). Then he slams her to the ground, and ties her legs together. Because he's being scored on his speed, he does this as fast as he can, without any regard for the living, feeling animal he's hurting.[112] Somehow, this is a sport—clotheslining baby animals, body slamming them, and then tying them up. And there are "judges" for this "sport," and it's considered "family entertainment." If this were being done to dogs, people would go postal. But there's a whole industry and audience comfortable with this because they're cows? Whether it's the calves, cows, horses, bulls, or broncos, there are countless instances of broken ribs, legs, and backs; ripped tendons; torn ligaments and muscles; deep internal organ bruising; hemorrhaging; punctured lungs; snapped necks; and deaths at the rodeo.[113] *Yeehaw.*

Why would anyone want to watch animals being dominated and injured by a bunch of insensitive, disconnected men who have confused notions of masculinity? Rodeos present themselves as fun, good-ol'-boys-kind of events. Maybe I'm missing something, but I'm not getting how these occurrences are "fun":

- A scared young horse burst screaming from the chutes, slammed into a fence, and broke her neck.

- By the end of one of the annual, nine-day Calgary Stampedes in Alberta, Canada, six animals were dead, including one horse who died of an aneurism and another who suffered a broken leg and had to be euthanized. The following year, six more animals died at the same event. Another year, fear caused a stampede as horses destined for the event were being herded across a bridge. Some jumped and others were pushed into the river, resulting in nine horse deaths.

- A horse crashed into a wall and broke his neck, and another horse broke his back after being forced to buck.

- A bull whose neck was broken during a steer-wrestling competition was left suffering for fifteen minutes before he was euthanized.[114]

- When the cowboys are done playing with their "toys," the abused, injured animals who are still alive are sent off to slaughter.[115] *We've had our fun with you, now we're gonna make a few bucks off you. And you're too mangled to fix anyway, partner.*

I don't know why there's this concept of cowboys being sexy. Is violence toward animals attractive to anyone? I'll take a card-carrying PETA member over a cowboy any day.

HORSE-DRAWN CARRIAGES

Maybe you're the sensitive type and wouldn't be caught dead at a rodeo. But you might consider a "romantic" horse-drawn carriage ride while on vacation. Many carriage horses are "break-downs" from racetracks.[116] Their bodies are already suffering from years of racing, and now they have to spend all day hauling a heavy carriage, bossy driver, and a bunch of tourists who don't know any better.

Many cities with carriages have no laws to protect the animals. And in cities that do have laws, they're not always enforced. Carriage rides in New York City are relentlessly romanticized in movies, but the horses there can be forced to work in the heat and cold nine hours a day, seven days a week.[117] Because the ASPCA Humane Law Enforcement Division may not always be around, some horses are worked even longer.[118] They pound the pavement with steel shoes on hot, hard asphalt, which is hell on their feet and legs and contributes to lameness.[119] And no greener pastures for these slaves—when they're not working, they "live" in multilevel stalls in the city and have to walk up steep ramps to the second story—more hell on their tired, arthritic feet and legs.[120] The law only requires that they're given sixty square feet of living space, despite the fact that experts recommend 144 square feet for standard breeds and 196 for larger breeds.[121] Experts also recommend that horses get turned out to pasture every day, or at least every few days. These horses never get turned out.[122] They live and work in New York City, and they never get to breathe fresh air. Imagine if you stood (not in your car, but on foot) in NYC traffic every day of your life. Of course the horses exhibit corresponding respiratory problems.[123]

Because of their docile demeanors, horses spook easily, which means accidents happen in nearly every city that allows horse carriages.[124] These can be fatal to the horses, and sometimes to the carriage drivers, passengers, and bystanders. Some of the accidents are cars crashing into the animals or the carriages. Other accidents are animals running into cars, structures, or people. And sometimes these poor, worn out animals just collapse.

When horses are no longer able to make money for humans, many are made into food for dogs or for carnivores in zoos, or shipped to countries where humans eat horsemeat. *How romantic.*

In a 2011 poll, *90* percent of respondents agreed that carriage rides should be banned.[125] And in Paris and London and other cities, they have been![126] The rest of the world needs to get with the program. Enough is enough already.

ACT III

LOST IN TRANSLATION

What if I told you that for twenty bucks, you could watch a group of men systematically torture and kill an animal? And that it's not meant to be some sicko snuff event, but something cool and fun and artistic? And that it's not at some underground venue, but something mainstream, legal, and celebrated? It would be totally shocking, right? And you'd likely want no part in it, right?

Since you're reading this book, chances are you're a dog lover and that you think of yourself as an animal lover. Yet many dog lovers/animal lovers will be the first in line when they travel to countries where bullfighting is a tradition. But they'll usually leave the event feeling sick, horrified, and deeply troubled. There's a general disconnect about what it is people think they're going to see at a bullfight. Without giving it much thought, they have this sense of, "I'm traveling to a land faraway; this is one of the activities offered by the travel guides; it'd be interesting to experience a part of the country's culture." Most people don't know that *matador* means *murderer* or *killer*. Literally. And that going to a bullfight means *we* are paying people to torture animals, then kill them—solely for *our* entertainment. Because we're in a different country, we justify it with words like "custom," "culture," and "tradition."

Details can vary from country to culture, but this is generally what happens at "traditional" bullfights: The "performance" is broken down into three parts. In the first part, the animal is forced into the ring and then teased, agitated, and antagonized by the matador with his colorful cape. Then two sidekicks on horseback enter. They lance the bull around his neck, trying to sever his neck muscles to make it harder for him to lift his head. This will make it easier later for the matador to stab the bull with his sword. The sidekicks do their best to gouge as deeply as possible, even twisting the lances to cause significant blood loss—they want to weaken and tire the bull so he's as defenseless as possible. To that effect, they also goad the bull, who, in his pain, anger, and frustration, will charge at the horses, often injuring them, sometimes fatally.

Part two. In come three men on foot, with *banderillas*, which are often described as colorful barbed darts, but look more like harpoons or spears. They stick them into the already suffering, exhausted bull. This further incites him, yet also weakens and injures him. They also run him in circles, dizzying him. (Sometimes, the matador will gouge the bull with his own banderillas.)

For the third and final part, the matador spends several minutes posing and posturing, swirling his cape at the bull, trying to bait the injured, weakened animal to charge. He also waves around a fake, lightweight sword, because it would be too tiring for him to wave around a real sword. He eventually swaps out his fake sword for a real sword, and tries to deliver a fatal blow between the bull's shoulders. Except more often than not, he's ineffective, and an executioner has to come in and try to stab the animal to death. It often takes multiple stabs. This, intrepid travelers, is bullfighting. *Olé.*

Check out some pictures online. It's truly heartbreaking. Researching this left me sick, angry, and devastated. The age-old excuse of "tradition" is given in a feeble attempt to justify bullfighting. As if "tradition" is so noble a concept, it cannot be argued with. Imagine all the sick stuff that would still exist in our culture if we used "tradition" as a defense—slavery, segregation, the criminalization of interracial marriages, women being the property of men, women not being allowed to vote, and child labor are just a few that come to mind.

If we have it in our hearts to feel compassion for dogs, surely we also have it in our hearts to feel compassion for bulls. Suffering is suffering. And tradition is not a valid excuse to harm others.

GET NAKED INSTEAD

Now's a good time to talk about the famed Running of the Bulls in Pamplona, Spain. This annual event attracts supposed thrill seekers, who want to feel the rush of danger running side by side with bulls. Guess where the Running of the Bulls ends? In a bullring. Guess what happens to the bulls in the bullring? They get killed. Guess whether running on slippery, narrow streets, with people yelling, hitting, and throwing things at them is fun for the bulls, who often fall and injure themselves? It's not. Sometimes I feel like I'm living in the Twilight Zone. How can people be so thoughtless and mean?

PETA has started an annual Running of the Nudes event (runningofthenudes.com) as an alternative to Running of the Bulls. I think that running naked through the streets in a crowd of animal lovers is a lot more courageous, liberating, and meaningful than running next to a bunch of senseless ogres trying to get a good picture of themselves to post on Facebook.

For a second, I just thought, "If you really want to face down a bull and feel the rush, do it in a natural environment somewhere wild." But forget that. God forbid we get our kicks without messing with animals. Why can't a bull just be left alone in a field, doing bull stuff? Why do we need to use him to get an adrenaline rush? We can bungee jump, skydive, hang glide, kite surf, and rock climb. We do not need to agitate animals for fun.

DOGS ON DRUGS

It's often assumed that greyhounds—who are fast, athletic, and agile—love to *race*. Make no mistake, greyhounds, like many dogs, love to *run*. But they only do it in short bursts, and then they're happy to lie on the couch or cuddle with their human. Neither of those are options for dogs used for racing. They live in constant confinement, in cages that are so small they can barely stand up or turn around. The only respite they get from imprisonment is when they are training or racing. They're like prison inmates, except these dogs didn't commit any crimes. But plenty of crimes are perpetrated against them, including the administering of steroids and other drugs, including cocaine.[127] They also suffer serious injuries like severed toes,[128] broken legs, broken necks, cardiac arrest, and spinal cord paralysis.[129]

When the dogs are deemed useless because they're injured, aren't winning, don't want to race, or are "too old" at eighteen months to five years, they either get killed or dumped at breeding facilities where they continue living in squalor and confinement.[130] Yes, some of them miraculously make it to rescue groups and then get placed in forever homes. But many don't. Unbelievably, dog racing is still legal in twelve states.[131]

I-KILLED-A-DOG

....

While greyhounds are toiling away on racetracks in the continental United States, Siberian huskies are being run to death in Alaska for the Iditarod race. The Iditarod is a 1,000-mile dogsled race across the most grueling and unforgiving terrain, in the most extreme weather conditions—temperatures as low as -50°F and winds up to 80 miles per hour. Personally, I'd rather eat a lightbulb, but I get that some people want to test their mettle, face the elements, and confront the challenge. What I can't get my head around is forcing dogs to bear the brunt of this decision. Iditarod dogs suffer from torn muscles, ripped up feet, dehydration, gastric erosion, intestinal viruses, pneumonia, bleeding ulcers, and respiratory issues. Of course, they can also die from good old-fashioned freezing to death, getting hit by a snowmobile, or a myriad of undiagnosed, unknown reasons. These dogs are as replaceable as greyhounds. Sled dogs are bred for the sole purpose of running fast and pulling sleds. If they don't measure up, they're *culled,* code for killed. One musher equates it to "weeding a garden."[132] *Yeah, 'cause dogs and weeds are totally the same.* Sportscaster Jim Rome aptly dubbed the Iditarod the "I-killed-a-dog." Sled dogs spend their lives in kennels or tethered, much like puppy-mill dogs spend their lives in cages.

CRUELTY YOU CAN BET ON

....

When I was in college at the University of Maryland, everyone would get all jazzed up over Preakness, an annual horse race in Baltimore. No one actually cared about the racing itself, they just wanted to have an opportunity to go somewhere and get drunk. When people would ask me why I wasn't going, I'd explain that I didn't think horses were put on this earth so I could be entertained by them or make money off them—and that Preakness, the Kentucky Derby, and all the other awful races were all the same. I'd then have to listen to a lot of misinformed, smug frat boys in annoying, know-it-all sounding voices say things like, "Race horses are treated better than most people treat their kids." Really? 'Cause I don't know any parents who allow people to beat their kids with crops, or who force their children to race around tracks at top speeds on hard-packed clay on their teeny, tiny ankles, way before their skeletal structure is finished developing, causing them fractures, strained tendons, and terrifying tumbles. I also don't know any parents who inject their kids with illegal drugs, or who ship them off to slaughter for dog food, glue, or meat for humans (Asia, South America, and Europe) when they can no longer race and make money for them.[133]

Just because women want an occasion to wear fancy hats and men want an excuse to wear seersucker suits and smoke cigars does not justify the exploitation and ultimate murder of these beautiful and innocent animals. Either people just don't know any better or it's the epitome of selfishness, shallowness, and senselessness. Surely we can find or invent other occasions to get drunk, smoke cigars, and wear big hats and seersucker.

LET'S KILL ANIMALS FOR FUN

Maybe seersucker isn't your thing but camouflage is. I don't understand how someone can love dogs and totally get their specialness, but then go out and murder animals who are equally special for "sport" or for a "trophy." Hunters,

I don't want to alienate you, really. I'm sorry to judge. It's just that the way you couldn't possibly imagine killing your dog for fun, I can't imagine that for any animal. The sadness you'd feel if your dog were injured or suffering, I feel that way about all animals. Suffering is suffering. Physical pain for a dog is physical pain for a deer. In suffering, we are all equal. Can you not find another way to enjoy your time that doesn't include hurting and killing animals? I've had conversations with hunters before. And even though it was difficult, I actively tried to be open and understanding. I can and did concede the following: I get that there is something primal and primordial about being part of the food chain and life cycle in such a physical, earthly way. I really do. But couldn't you just go for a hike, instead? Or build something from trees and leaves and vines? It seems to me that your fleeting enjoyment of the "sport" of hunting is an unfair and imbalanced trade for the entire life of an animal. I beg you to reconsider your position—to really try on a new possibility that these animals are here for their own reasons, that they want to live, and that your pleasure doesn't justify their death. I fully agree with Alice Walker, who said, "The animals of the world exist for their own reasons. They were not made for humans any more than black people were made for white, or women created for men."

If you're a regular civilian who doesn't hunt, but thinks hunters are the salt of the earth, there are some things you should know. For starters, hunting disturbs hibernation and migration patterns.[134] Also, hunting isn't an exact science: It's estimated that for every animal killed and recovered by a hunter, at least two wounded but unrecovered animals die of blood loss, infection, or starvation.[135] Slowly and painfully.[136] The ones who don't die are often left disabled by their injuries. Some hunters—to increase the "challenge" of killing animals—hunt with a bow and arrow. One study found that *half* of the animals shot using traditional archery equipment were wounded but not recovered by the hunters.[137] Imagine if you lived deep in the woods, were shot with an arrow, and weren't able to go to a doctor or hospital for help. You'd either have to live with your wound/injury, or succumb to it. Also, hunters kill mommy animals, which means orphaned babies who will either starve to death or become easy prey. Some animals, like geese and wolves, form long-term pair bonds like humans. Hunters don't spare animals who seem happily mated.

So spare me the propaganda about how hunting helps with population control or how animals would starve to death if not for hunters. Every year in the United States, hunters kill forty-two million mourning doves, thirty million squirrels, twenty-eight million quail, twenty-five million rabbits, twenty million pheasants, fourteen million ducks, six million deer, and thousands of geese, bears, moose, elk, antelope, swans, cougars, turkeys, wolves, foxes, coyotes, bobcats, boars, and other woodland creatures.[138] The white-tailed deer that hunters talk about when referring to overpopulation make up only *3 percent* of the animals killed annually.[139] The rest of the animals aren't overpopulated; thousands are even natural predators of the white-tail deer. So where's the logic? The answer: *there is no logic.* Just a smokescreen so hunters can kill can animals and the U.S. Fish and Wildlife Services can sell licenses.

Mother Nature does not need humans to sort out animal populations. Humans are the most overpopulated species on the planet. Perhaps we should focus on our own population problem instead of pretending to be so concerned with the deer.

We're the reason they're out of control to begin with. The deer population would likely be stable today if livestock farmers hadn't killed so many wolves a hundred years ago. Regardless, there's evidence that deer hunting has actually caused an *increase* of deer numbers. In hunted populations, does have been reproducing at younger ages and are more likely to have twins than a single fawn.[140] Also, right after a hunt, there's less competition for food, so survivors are better nourished, which can mean higher reproductive rates and lower neonatal death rates.[141] So in the long term, we've now got more deer than before, and less food. So instead of helping starvation, hunting can actually cause it.[142] (P.S.—It's not like sport hunters are stalking starving deer.[143] In all those disturbing photos of hunters posing over their dead victims, you never see one beaming with pride over a frail, malnourished, starving, knocking-on-death's-door deer. They shoot animals at random, or they seek out the biggest ones so they have impressive "trophies" to hang on their walls.)[144]

Also bogus is the claim that hunting helps with "wildlife management" and "conservation." The New Jersey Division of Fish, Game and Wildlife has stated that, "the deer resource has been managed primarily for the purpose of sport hunting."[145]

Hunting also means more danger for humans, and I'm not even talking about hunting accidents. After analyzing deer-vehicle collision data for more than a decade, a Pennsylvania-based insurance company found that opening day and the first Saturday of the deer hunting season are "two of the most dangerous days to drive."[146] Interestingly, though, hunters often cite deer-vehicle accidents as another reason to kill more deer.[147]

In the United States, hunting is permitted in 60 percent of wildlife refuges.[148] Um, you don't need to be a literary scholar to know that, by its very definition, a *refuge* is meant to be a safe haven. What the hell? Hunting's also allowed in many state parks and national forests; more than

200 million animals are killed annually on federal land alone—over half a billion acres.[149] I find this disturbing and disgusting. Even though hunters make up less than 7 percent of the population, they maim and kill millions of animals every year on public land.[150] (It's estimated that unlicensed hunters are killing just as many illegally.)[151] And even though that percentage may not seem like a lot, the money they spend on hunting licenses makes them an important demographic for national forests and state parks. To the degree that federal and state agencies actively recruit kids to start hunting early in life, knowing that killing animals isn't something most people take up once they're adults.[152] Some agencies have even gotten schools to offer hunting courses.[153] Seriously. Talk about conflict of interest; the very same agencies that are responsible for protecting and conserving wildlife are the very same agencies that are trying to breed hunters for dollars. Because hunters are more likely to buy licenses in subsequent years if previous hunts were successful, wildlife agencies also implement "management" or "conservation" programs designed to boost popular "game" species.[154] Not only is it unfair and unsportsmanlike, it's also dangerous: The epidemic spread of chronic wasting disease (CWD), a fatal neurological sickness that resembles mad cow disease, is believed to have been caused by the transfer of captive-bred deer and elk between states (so hunters can kill them).[155]

Sounds like a clear case of the fox guarding the henhouse, right? Wildlife agencies are partially funded by the sale of hunting licenses and by excise taxes on hunting equipment and fishing gear.[156] So even though hunters are a minority population, they have a disproportionate say in how wildlife is managed.[157] The other 93 percent of us who actually treasure and revere wildlife (and pay taxes, which go to these wildlife agencies) have little to no say.[158] I present this as Exhibit A for "Why animal lovers need to be politically active."

Before donating money to a so-called wildlife or conservation group, find out what their position is on hunting. Shockingly, some groups are in favor of sport-hunting (or they do not oppose it), including the National Wildlife Federation, the National Audubon Society, the Sierra Club, the Wilderness Society, and the World Wildlife Fund.[159] (*I'm blowing raspberries at them right now.*)

TORTURE AND RELEASE

What about "sport" fishing? Fish certainly don't invoke in us the same emotion that zebras or giraffes do. And they aren't cute and cuddly. For those reasons alone, it's easy to remain a little detached from the plight of fish. That, and the multibillion dollar fishing industry has done a great job perpetuating the myth that fish don't feel pain. Multiple studies by leading scientists and universities have proven time and time again and in a multitude of ways: *Fish do feel pain.* Say it out loud so you don't forget it: *Fish do feel pain.* In studying the pain receptors of fish, researchers from the University of Edinburgh and University of Glasgow found that theirs were strikingly similar to those of mammals: "Fish do have the capacity for pain perception and suffering."[160] John Webster, Professor Emeritus of Animal Husbandry of the University of Bristol's Department of Clinical Veterinary Science, puts it brilliantly: "To say that a fish cannot feel pain because it doesn't have a neocortex is like saying it cannot breathe because it doesn't have lungs."[161]

World-renowned animal behaviorist Jonathan Balcombe, PhD, explains how "their relative lack of facial expression" is a possible explanation for why fish are falsely yet "commonly denied feeling" by humans.[162]

> When they are impaled on a hook, fish don't scream or grimace, though their gaping mouths may evoke a look of shock or horror to the empathetic witness. Using facial expression as a guide for sentience is hardly valid when one considers that some of the most intelligent and highly sentient marine vertebrates—namely the dolphins and whales—also lack facial expression, at least any that most of us can readily detect. However, animals have many other ways of visually signaling their feelings. Crests, dewlaps, mouth-pages, pupil dilation and contraction, color changes, and body postures and movements are among the many visual ways fish and other animals convey emotions.[163]

Imagine if you were scuba diving and you ran out of air. When fish are yanked from the water, they run out of air and they suffocate. Their gills often collapse, and their swim bladders can rupture from the sudden change in pressure.[164] They're also extremely stressed. According to Professor Culum Brown of Macquarie University, the stress hormones of fish being pulled from the water are "exactly the same as a person drowning."[165] That's all in addition to having a sharp, multipronged metal hook ripping the flesh of their mouths and being roughly handled by anglers who think they don't feel any pain. (I guess that explains why some fishermen just tear the hooks out of the fishes' faces.) None of this makes "catch and release" look like a humane practice. Ultimately, many catch-and-release fish will die shortly after their release anyway. One study found that as many as 43 percent of released fish died within six days.[166] After being caught, they can have damage to their fins and mouths, a dangerous buildup of lactic acid in their muscles, oxygen depletion, and loss in scale coating, which makes them more vulnerable to disease.[167] Their numbers are also in peril—according to one study, sport fishermen are responsible for killing nearly 25 percent of overfished saltwater species.[168] Because of overfishing, many trout streams have a catch-and-release policy, which means these poor fish can spend their entire lives being repeatedly traumatized and injured, all for someone's hobby. [169]

My friend Lance used to go on an annual deep-sea fishing trip with his buddies. One year, he got a 200-pound tuna on his line. For hours, this fish fought for his life, and Lance fought to land him in the boat. The battle finally ended and the fish was lying on the deck, suffocating, struggling for his last few breaths. Lance looked down at him, into his eye that was "as big as a dinner plate," and realized, "I don't need to do this anymore." He saw the humanity in the fish, and the lack of humanity in himself. He never fished again. And he never ate another fish again, either. In fact, he became a vegan from then on.

By the way, it isn't just the fish who suffer from fishing. Every year in the United States alone, over a million birds and 100,000 marine mammals die from "ingestion of and entanglement in marine debris."[170] Manatees, dolphins, turtles, and every type of marine bird imaginable. My friend Zoli does pelican rescue work in California. Every single bird he helps is either wrapped in fishing line, has a hook embedded in his or her flesh, or both. Every single one.

I know everyone will have sympathy for the manatees, dolphins, turtles, and birds, but what about the sharks? It's estimated that 100 million sharks are killed every year.[171] The shark fin trade is going strong, despite how cruelly its product is procured. Whether it's for shark fin soup or Chinese "medicine," sharks are brutally attacked for their fins. Fishermen will catch sharks, hack off their fins, then toss the animals back into the water. Shark "meat" isn't valuable; fisherman don't want to waste space on the boat. They just want the fins. After being tossed back into the water, sharks will either bleed to death, suffocate, drown, starve to death, or be attacked and killed by other predators. Animal lovers in Asia, we need you to get loud up in here! This has to stop.

KILLING CONTESTS

When these majestic animals aren't being brutalized for their fins, they're being brutalized for fun. Because we're scared of them, sharks have become the bad guys of the ocean. So somehow, it's become acceptable to have shark tournaments. There are actual fishing contests where the objective is to go out and kill sharks. Whoever kills the biggest shark wins. When did fraternities take over the world? If we stopped for just a moment to consider that these are living, breathing, feeling beings—if we didn't allow our shark adrenaline to take over, because let's face it, sharks are exciting—would we even tolerate, let alone *celebrate*, these disgusting contests? Sharks that don't meet the size requirements of contests are hooked, wrestled with for what can be hours, and then thrown back in. Who cares about injuring a shark and making them fight for their lives. They're mean and scary-looking, right? Of course, none of the participants know the sizes of the sharks the other participants are catching, so lots of sharks are killed for the "game," whether they're "winners" or not.

Obviously, they're all losers, and so are we because sharks are a vital part of the marine ecosystem. As *apex* (top) predators, sharks target the sick or weak fish and marine animals, which means survival of the fittest and a healthy gene pool for survivors. In messing with the sharks, we threaten to destabilize the whole ecosystem. And my God, we have messed with the sharks: their numbers have declined a staggering 90 percent worldwide![172] We are so scared of sharks, and yet in 2011, there were only twelve fatal shark attacks on humans.[173] Humans kill more than 270,000 sharks *every single day*, which of course is pushing many species to the edge of extinction.[174] But they're the bad guys? Also, how many fish are killed just for chumming the waters to catch sharks? On top of the senseless waste, we're also conditioning sharks that boats mean food for them, which is not so great for those of us who like to swim off boats.

Why are these tournaments legal? How are people allowed to arbitrarily murder a bunch of animals in this world we all live in together and are all stewards of? Don't the rest of us nonkillers get a say? Yeah, the contest organizers profit off these events, but so do the communities that host them. Hotels and inns get filled up; restaurants get patronized; and stores sell their wares. What if the elected officials of these towns had integrity about how they were drumming up business? What if business owners announced that they wanted no part of this blood money, and together, they figured out another way to attract tourists? When there are no more sharks left to attract shark-killers, will they close up shop or figure out a new way to thrive? Well, the time is always right to do the right thing.

CHAPTER 9

WHO ARE YOU WEARING?

WINTER COLLECTION

I'm fortunate to have the most beautiful group of friends, most of whom live their lives as a testament to compassion. One of them is Shannon Mann, who you may know from Animal Planet's *Whale Wars*. Shannon's been on multiple campaigns with Sea Shepherd to help stop the killing of whales, sharks, dolphins, seals, bluefin tuna, and other marine life. But what many people don't know is that Shannon's a dedicated activist on land, too. She regularly organizes events, coordinates rescues of domestic and wild animals, assists with investigations, attends protests for circuses, zoos, rodeos, stores selling fur, the Canadian seal hunt, and anything else that warrants protesting.

In addition to all her other amazingness, Shannon's also actively involved with three animal rescue groups in Canada. Clarissa, a friend she does rescues with, was in Los Angeles with Shannon when she and I got together recently. They told me how just before they left Canada to visit L.A., they had spent the day trying to catch a dog who had a fur trap attached to her leg. Shannon and her angelic cohorts were successful in their daylong efforts, thankfully. But all animals aren't as fortunate.

FUR IS NOT IN FASHION

In the wild, animals are caught by snares, body grip traps, and steel-jawed leghold traps. Steel-jawed leghold traps are those metal clamps with teeth that fur trappers set out in the wild to catch fur-bearing animals. When they come upon animals they've caught who are still alive, trappers kill them by shooting them, stomping on them, or beating their skulls in. Can you imagine how you'd feel if you were out hiking and you came across an animal, mutilated, but still alive, caught in a trap? Can you imagine if you were out hiking with your dog and she stepped on a trap? It happens. The trappers may have their sights set on a particular species—like fox, mink, rabbit, raccoon, or coyote—but any animal passing by can step into the trap. (Kids can, too.) Beloved pets and stray dogs, like the one Shannon and Clarissa rescued, get caught in traps all the time. Sometimes it's a limb that gets caught, other times it's their faces, because they were sniffing the trap. Trappers sometimes don't check their traps for days, so animals caught in the trap can slowly bleed to death, starve to death, freeze to death, or bake to death. Or, trapped and defenseless, they can be killed by a wild predator. Or they can bleed to death after chewing off their trapped limb.

The world was riveted by the James Franco movie, *127 Hours*, based on the true story of Aron Ralston. Ralston, who was hiking alone, got his forearm caught between a boulder and canyon wall and, in order to save his own life, had to cut off his arm. This story is compelling for so many reasons; I don't begrudge anyone that. But every year, *countless* animals chew off limbs so humans can wear fur—and it goes virtually unnoticed.

Also unnoticed are fur farms. Eighty-five percent of animals killed for their fur come from fur factory farms.[175] Thousands of animals are crammed into cages, barely able to move, covered in urine, feces, and festering wounds. They're executed by strangulation, drowning, gassing, poisoning, neck-breaking, and anal or vaginal electrocution. You read right: anal or vaginal electrocution. Have you ever heard a rabbit screaming? It's totally in right now.

Some people who wear fur may even call themselves "animal lovers." They may have a hard time feeling sympathy for wild animals, but actually care about domestic ones, like dogs and cats. What they don't know is that dogs and cats are also part of the fur trade. Manufacturers will deliberately mislabel their products so consumers would never know they were buying dog and cat fur.

I've seen photos and video footage of the dog and cat fur trade in China. It's agonizing and unbearable. Cats and dogs are stuffed into these small, flat cages. When I say stuffed, I mean stuffed—there are so many per cage and they are so crammed in, it's hard to tell where one animal stops and another animal begins. When I say flat, I mean that the height of the cages are so low, the animals are grossly folded over themselves and each other. The cages are thin metal or wire; there are many, and they're stacked on top of one another in the backs of trucks. Thousands of squished dogs and cats on top of other squished dogs and cats. A few faces were visible in the blur of wire and fur. I'm still haunted by them. I felt like I would go insane just watching them so restricted, and I'm crying now just remembering it. The devastating confinement in itself was unforgettably horrible. But then the men in the video started tossing the cages from the top of the pile to the ground, ten feet below. Like they were just tossing cardboard boxes. It's video footage like this that changes a person from an animal lover to an animal rights activist.

So as an activist, and not just a dog and cat lover, I ask: Does it need to be a dog or cat for us to feel compassion? Like it only matters if it's animals "we know?" Suffering is suffering, whether it's a mink, a rabbit (angora is made from rabbits, FYI), or a kitten. Ingrid Newkirk, cofounder and president of PETA said it best: "When it comes to pain, love, joy, loneliness, and fear, a rat is a pig is a dog is a boy. Each one values his or her life and fights the knife."

And if you value the planet, you'll ditch fur. Every year just in the United States, mink farms alone produce one million pounds of excrement. This means nearly a thousand tons of phosphorous, polluting rivers and streams.[176]

FALL COLLECTION

WHOSE SKIN ARE YOU IN?

Eschewing fur is probably an easy swallow for most people; it's not hard to see how unnecessary and cruel it is. But a lot of people who are anti-fur don't even consider that they're wearing dead animals on their feet (shoes), around their waists (belts), in their pockets (wallets), and slung over their shoulders (bags). *Whoops.* These objects sold in stores—bought and worn without a second's thought—are the skins of animals. Leather or suede can come from cows, chickens, pigs, goats, sheep, alligators, snakes, sharks, ostriches, kangaroos, and even dogs and cats. Yep, in China, it's estimated that two million dogs and cats are killed every year for their skins,[177] which the Chinese export globally. Your favorite dog-walking shoes that you wear every day to take Fido out could be made from another Fido. You'd never know because these products are intentionally mislabeled.[178] Regardless of whether it's dog leather, cat leather, or cow leather, now's the time to realize that the collar you bought for one animal is made from another animal. China is the world's leading leather exporter, India is the second largest.

India surprised me because I'd always heard that cows are sacred there. Indeed, they are, but as it often does, the almighty dollar (or rupee) trumps all that is sacred. In direct violation of the Constitution of India, laws that protect cows are either circumvented, ignored, or unenforced.[179] Cows are marched and driven from the Hindu states to the Islamic states for slaughter, and go days without food and sometimes even a day or more without water in the excruciating Indian heat.[180] When they collapse from injury or exhaustion, in order to get them moving again, workers will smear chili pepper and tobacco into their eyes and break their tails.[181] Dead on their feet, these poor beings have to be dragged into slaughterhouses, where once inside, their throats are slashed—often with dull, dirty knives and in full view of one another.[182] Sometimes, these "sacred" animals are even skinned and dismembered while still conscious.[183]

If you're thinking, "Oh, my shoes were made in Italy or the United States, so those animals weren't mistreated," think again. First of all, the "raw materials" (skins) were most likely from China or India. Secondly, animals who are raised and killed to make money for humans usually aren't well treated, regardless of their country of origin. In the United States, where we supposedly have "strong" animal protection laws, we have cows being skinned and dismembered, sometimes while fully conscious, struggling and bellowing in terror.[184]

It isn't just animals who suffer from the leather trade. The leather tanning process is one of the worst chemical polluters in the world.[185] We need to remember that leather is the decomposing skin of a dead animal. In order to keep it from rotting away like roadkill, a lot needs to be done to it. There are so many phases of the process, all of which include a different batch of chemicals—pretreatment of the raw skins, the tanning treatment, bleaching, dyeing, weaving, finishing, and shining. In addition to a boatload of other chemicals, the majority of the industry uses toxic chromium compounds for tanning. Rinsing the skins creates a lot of waste, which is filled with chemicals, chromium compounds, skins, hide scraps, and excess fat.[186] And all this solid waste and wastewater leaches into nearby soil and surface-and groundwater, wreaking environmental havoc and causing devastating health problems for the local communities. Every year in Hazaribagh, a tanning region of Bangladesh, 7.7 million liters (two million gallons) of wastewater and eighty-eight million tons of solid waste are dumped.[187] (This is just in one region of the world and just for one year!) The toxic chromium can get into air, soil, food, and water—causing respiratory ailments; affecting all the crops, marine life, and farm animals, whom people eat; and damaging all the cooking, bathing, and drinking water.[188]

Inhalation among workers has been found to cause respiratory cancers, eye damage, ulcerations, swelling, asthmatic bronchitis, irritation to the throat and nose, and holes in the nasal septum.[189] Nearby residents who ingest the chromium via food and water suffer from ulcers, kidney and liver problems, stomach issues, and anemia. Skin exposure can cause rashes, sores, and ulcers.[190]

Incidence of leukemia was found to be *five times* the national average near one tannery in Kentucky.[191] *Twenty years* after another United States tannery closed down, groundwater samples revealed that arsenic, lead, chromium, and zinc are still present. Samples taken from a nearby river and its wetlands indicated the presence of cyanide, chromium, and polychlorinated biphenyls (PCBs)![192] This stuff is no joke. It's messing up the planet.

Our desire to wear or own leather products translates into animals killed, environmental destruction, and human suffering. It's understandable if you never made the connection before, but now that you know and have been educated, what will you do? Will you turn off this knowing the next time you want to buy something made from an animal and find a way to justify the purchase? If you have to numb out or check out to be okay with it, what does that say? How do you think you'll feel every time you use it or wear it?

When I was in college, Birkenstocks were all the rage. For months, I had been searching for the perfect pair. I was so excited when I finally found *the* pair. They were the perfect color, style, and fit, and I was over the moon that I had held out for so long. Until I realized that they were leather. When I started the search, I didn't know anything about leather. But by the time I found *the* pair, I had seen the light and sworn off animal skins. In that moment, I was faced with an important decision. Do what I knew was right, or do what I wanted? I didn't know it then, but I was forging my destiny in that very moment. I was either going to be someone with integrity who stood by my beliefs—even when it meant not getting what I wanted—or I was going to buy the shoes "just this one time" (because I'd been searching for so long and they were the *perfect* pair) and start being someone with integrity later. I am proud to say that I did not buy the shoes that day. It was painful, and I was mad that I couldn't have what I wanted. But obviously, I know I made the right choice. Had I bought the shoes, I'm not sure who I'd be today.

If you find yourself in a similar situation and you need help doing the right thing, I *strongly suggest* watching the powerful three-minute, "Whose Skin are You In?"

Don't get all freaked out that you'll be some hemp-wearing hippie— there are plenty of nonleather jackets, belts, wallets, shoes, and purses that look like leather, but are man-made or synthetic. You'll figure it out. Honestly, it's not that hard. You can still be fashion-forward *and* be compassionate.

HOME COLLECTION

HOUSE OF HORRORS

You can extend this compassion to your home decorating, too. It's unbearable seeing all those animal-skin rugs that are so popular right now. How disconnected are we that we toss the skins of dead horses, zebras, sheep, and cows on the floor so haplessly, and think it's attractive and stylish? Or that we buy couches and armchairs made entirely of dead cows? They could just as easily be dog-skin rugs or cat-skin chairs. Why is it okay? It's not. It's not okay. And hanging the heads of dead animals on the walls is in such bad taste. Would you hang a dog's head? No, so why is a deer's head "rustic" or "homey"? It isn't; *it's gross*. And so is other taxidermy. The whole "hunting lodge" motif is so tired, passé, and completely uninspired. If your decorator wants to throw down a bear rug or hang up a dear's head, he or she needs a mental makeover.

I'M NOT DOWN WITH DOWN

Yes, down comforters, pillows, and jackets are soft, warm, and cozy. But they come at a price to innocent birds. Many farmers aren't waiting for ducks and geese to go through natural molting phases to shed their feathers. They're ripping the feathers from their bodies every six weeks, from the time the birds are ten weeks old until they're four years old.[193] This practice, called *live plucking*, often leaves birds with gaping wounds and even kills them.

(Sometimes workers will do a crude sewing job on the wounds—without any anesthesia, of course.) The animals, who are either shrieking in terror or paralyzed with fear, are usually held upside down, squeezed between the workers' legs. One investigation revealed a worker sitting on a goose's neck.[194] Most birds exploited for their down are also used for meat or foie gras production. *Foie gras* means fatty liver in French, and it's considered a delicacy by people who are either ignorant, disconnected, or both. In order to produce this fatty liver, a feeding tube or pipe is forced down the birds' throats, and they are force-fed.

There are so many synthetic alternatives for down. And even if there weren't, it's abhorrent to continue propagating this practice.

SPRING COLLECTION

DON'T PULL THE WOOL OVER YOUR EYES
....

I'm sure you don't want to hear this, but wool production also means suffering for animals. Contrary to popular belief, sheep don't need to be sheared. When left untouched, as nature intended, they grow just the right amount of wool to regulate their temperature and insulate against both the heat and the cold. However, sheep have now been genetically manipulated to grow more wool so farmers can make more money.

Merino wool, which is the majority of wool coming out of Australia, comes from sheep who are bred to have wrinkled skin, so that more wool can grow in the wrinkles. *(Ridiculous, right?)* An inherent problem with these wrinkles is that they can collect urine and moisture, attracting flies. These flies then lay eggs in the skin folds, causing what's called "flystrike"—and the hatched maggots can potentially eat the sheep alive. So how do the farmers combat this flystrike? By mulesing. Mulesing is a practice that has farmers chopping off a dinner-plate sized chunk of the sheep's flesh or carving strips of flesh off the sheep's tail area and legs.[195] Of course, this is done without anesthesia or painkillers of any kind. The intention is to create smooth, scarred skin so that the flies won't have anywhere to lay eggs. But the flies often attack the open wound before it has time to heal.

Sadly, the abuse and horror starts way before mulesing. Only weeks after being born, baby lambs have their tails chopped off, holes punched into their ears, and their testicles removed. It's commonplace for hundreds of babies to die every year from starvation or exposure, and for mature sheep to perish from disease, neglect, and lack of shelter.[196] Workers hired to shear the animals aren't usually paid by the hour, they're paid by the volume of wool they reap. So it benefits them to work fast, which often means carelessly and callously. One witness said, "[T]he shearing shed must be one of the worst places in the world for cruelty to animals. . . . I have seen shearers punch sheep with their shears or their fists until the sheep's nose bled. I have seen sheep with half their faces shorn off. . . ."[197]

If the lambs make it into adulthood and then survive disease, neglect, abuse, multiple shearings, and exposure, millions are then shipped off to the Middle East and North Africa, where they'll be killed for their flesh. These trips, known as live exports, have animals crowded onto multilevel export ships, where they'll sometimes remain for weeks. Australia has been exporting sheep to the Middle East since 1981.[198] Hundreds of millions have been subjected to this miserable voyage, with up to 2 percent not surviving the long, arduous journey. So for thirty years, millions of dead and dying sheep have been thrown overboard.[199] Since they're going to be killed upon arrival, they are not well treated, fed, watered, or otherwise cared for en route. Understandably, after weeks of neglect and travel, many are unable to walk off the ship to be loaded onto trucks, so they're forcibly dragged by their ears or legs.[200] And as if their lives hadn't been hard enough, some are driven miles and miles away, forcibly dragged off the trucks and into slaughterhouses, where they can have their throats stabbed open while they're still conscious.[201] Others are left to die in barren feedlots.[202] And others are tied up and tossed into car trunks, like old suitcases.[203] Whether it's wool, cashmere, mohair, pashmina, alpaca, or shearling, it's from an animal. You don't have to throw it all in the trash, but from now on you can buy cruelty-free alternatives, instead.

And you can feel good knowing you're not jacking up the planet. Raising hundreds of millions of sheep comes at a huge cost to the planet in terms of erosion, land degradation, increased soil salinity, reduced biodiversity, depletion of resources, and pollution. After studying land degradation in South Africa, Oxford researchers reported that large numbers of farmed animals, especially sheep, caused erosion and an unfavorable change in vegetation that led to the formation of gullies and badlands (heavily eroded, barren areas).[204]

Patagonia, Argentina, used to be second to Australia in wool production. But sheep farming caused soil deterioration, triggering desertification. In one province alone, over fifty million acres have been irrevocably damaged.[205]

Like leather processing, wool production not only uses huge amounts of water, it also uses huge amounts of chemicals,[206] which pollute water. In one region of Wales, pollution from sheep dip pesticides were linked to a major decline in invertebrates.[207]

And of course, manure generated by sheep contributes to global warming. In New Zealand, methane from grazing animals, including sheep, makes up about half of its greenhouse gas emissions.[208]

It's not that big a deal to change your ways. Before buying something, just ask yourself: did this come from an animal? Yeah, shopping may take a little more effort. And in the beginning, it may feel like a "sacrifice" not getting what you want. But when you acknowledge that not having a jacket, wallet, purse, belt, rug, blanket, sweater, or pair of shoes isn't a big sacrifice—compared to environmental destruction; the poisoning of humans; and animals being imprisoned, tortured, and slaughtered—things start to shift. Forgoing what you want for the greater good builds self-esteem. And it builds a rarely used spiritual muscle, too.

CHAPTER 10

CH-CH-CH-CHANGES

PART I: THE ANIMALS

C hange is hard. Most of us resist it with everything we've got. But if we don't change, we don't grow. When you're done with this chapter, you'll have options:

- You can disagree with me and use that as a reason not to change.

- You can resent me and this book, and use it as an excuse not to change.

- You can feel the intense discomfort knowing that the opportunity to change is upon you and fail to meet the challenge.

- You can feel the intense discomfort or excitement knowing that the opportunity to change is upon you and rise up to meet the challenge.

You can do it with fear and dread, or with vim and vigor. It doesn't matter; change is hard. Some of us walk through fire with dignity and grace; others do it kicking and screaming. As long as you're walking through it and not resisting change, you're growing. I've had my fair share of tantrums and brat-attacks around change. It wasn't pretty. In fact, it's been pretty ugly at times. But I've never regretted change. Even when it was painful. Even when it was scary. Even when it was a lot of work. And even though I've changed a lot, it's a job that's never done. I've still got changes to make. Some I'm clear on and actively working through; others are those I haven't yet met, but I know they're out there. I hope I never stop changing and growing. And I hope you'll join me on the path so we can be bratty or graceful together.

Okay, so here goes:

In recent years, there's been a lot of attention paid to the slaughter of whales and dolphins by Japanese whalers and fishermen. When we watch shows like *Whale Wars* or see Oscar-award-winning movies like *The Cove*, we all go ballistic. And rightly so. What's been—and is still being—done to these animals is a monumental horror, and there should be a public outcry. It varies by account, but the number of whales and dolphins killed each year is approximately 30,000. Of course, this is 30,000 too many, and thanks to the many individuals and animal rights groups who work tirelessly on these issues, this number has declined from where it once was—and hopefully it'll soon reach zero. But in the justified outrage over the killing of dolphins and whales, most people fail to see is that there is a holocaust happening every single day in their own countries—and worse, that they are a part of it.

Sadly, 30,000 is a pittance compared to the number of other animals killed each year for human consumption. You may not eat whale or dolphin meat, but chances are you eat other meat. By low estimates, worldwide, 150 billion animals are killed each year for food.[209] 150 billion. Every single year. Is this not staggering?

The top three consumers of animal products are the United States, China, and Brazil—making up more than 46 percent of the world's consumption.[210] And even though we make up only 5 percent of the world's population, Americans eat more than 20 percent of the animals killed.[211] I used to very much be your average American.

During my senior year of high school, every day for breakfast I had Taylor ham, egg, and cheese on a roll; for lunch, a bacon double cheeseburger. And dinner was almost always some meat, chicken, or fish. I'm from New Jersey—vegetarianism just wasn't on my radar at all. I ate meat for every single meal, every single day.

I was also your average American animal lover. I grew up with a dog and cats and birds. I never realized the disparity between being a so-called animal lover and an ardent meat eater. How could I possibly have made the connection when "meat" is so carefully marketed and packaged as anything but a dead, rotting, decomposing carcass of an animal who's been slaughtered?

When I was a freshman at the University of Maryland, I met Tracy Silverman. (I talked about her earlier in the zoo section. She's the one who wants her daughters to be nice.) We initially bonded over unfortunate hair, but quickly became BFFs over more meaningful traits. Like me, Tracy was an animal lover. Unlike me, Tracy was a vegetarian. I'd never met one before. She was like a unicorn. Even though I was vexed that her animal lover-ness trumped mine, it didn't even occur to me that I could or should be a vegetarian, too. Without thinking, I responded, "Oh, I could never be a vegetarian. I love meat too much." Case closed. Because Tracy is a model of love and acceptance, she never shamed me for my utter disconnect or hypocrisy. But clearly, a seed had been planted.

About a year later, I was in my off-campus apartment on Guilford Drive. I had gotten an animal magazine in the mail, probably because I had donated twenty bucks to some dog or cat charity that sold my address. The magazine was from PETA. I had never heard of them, but I remember the whole event like it was yesterday. I was sitting at the table, my unfortunate hair piled atop my head with a big scrunchy. (I also had bangs, just so you know.) I was casually leafing through the magazine, but then felt compelled to stop. There was an article, with pictures, about factory farming and slaughterhouses. I had never seen a family farm, let alone heard of a *factory* farm.

The same way puppy mills are large-scale breeding operations for dogs, factory farms are large-scale breeding operations for animals we eat (or take milk and eggs from). The idea is to raise as many animals as possible, in as small an area as possible, as cheaply as possible. Except they aren't considered animals like you and I consider animals. They're considered "units" or "production units." Commodities. Goods to sell for dollars. If you're thinking Old MacDonald Had a Farm, erase that vision completely, because factory farming is its antithesis.

THIS LITTLE PIGGY . . .

Raise your hand if you cried when you read *Charlotte's Web* or saw the movie, or when you watched *Babe*. My hand is up; I bawled my eyes out. But neither made me cry as much as the plight of pigs in real life. From start to finish, these animals have it worse than any character in a book or movie.

Piglets are taken away from their moms as young as ten days old.[212] Before deciding who will be used to breed and who will be used for their flesh, farmers overcrowd them into pens with one another, which is so stressful they can resort to tail biting or cannibalism.[213] So farmers will cut off the piglets' tails and, using pliers, break off the ends of their teeth.[214] In some countries, including the United States, they also rip or cut off their testicles so consumers don't complain of "boar taint" from their sex pheromones.[215] If you Google "Mercy for Animals Pig Abuse," you'll see piglets struggling futilely in desperate terror and hear them squealing in pain. But their lives never get any better once they get older. Well, actually, they don't even get much older. Without human interference, they can live up to fifteen years. But once they reach "market weight"—about 250 pounds—they're referred to as "hogs" and slaughtered at around six months.[216]

More than 80 percent of sows—pregnant pigs—are confined to the degree that they can't even turn around.[217] Can you even imagine being nine months pregnant, trapped in one position, totally unable to move?! Of course it's maddening. Literally. Like animals in zoos, they exhibit neurotic, obsessive behaviors like bar biting, sham chewing (chewing nothing), and head banging.[218] Not only are they imprisoned and stuck in one position, but they're in a crate with no straw. Their nesting instincts are so strong they'll sometimes rub their snouts raw on the floor trying to satisfy the biological urge.[219] Once their babies are taken from them, they're impregnated again, and the process continues. They are literally baby-making machines. After a lifetime of servitude; constant confinement; and a perpetual cycle of insemination, pregnancy, birthing, and having their babies torn away from them—when their "production" starts to slow down, after about three or four years—they're slaughtered.[220] *That'll do, pig. That'll do.*

On my computer one night, I was watching an author give a speech about orgasms. It was interesting—until she mentioned that pig farmers found a way to increase pig fertility. Then it got perverse. It's believed that females have more piglets if they achieve orgasm during artificial insemination. I don't know if pigs orgasm, and if they do, how farmers figured out that it increases offspring. Regardless, the author showed an instructional video made by farmers to demonstrate the technique. A female pig is eating hay and a male worker enters her pen. He starts massaging her udders, rubbing her back and sides, squeezing her nipples, and sticking his fingers inside her vagina. He also presses her back and climbs on top of her. All of this is done to simulate the boar who would copulate with her. While on top of her, the worker inserts the syringe of boar semen inside her. I watched the video in utter horror and disbelief. But the author was showing the video with delight and the audience was squealing with laughter. A man is sexually stimulating a female pig, playing the role of the male pig, and then inseminating her with boar semen. This is funny? No, it's *bestiality*. But humans inseminating animals is often a standard part of industrialized farming. It's yet another dirty little secret of meat production. Want one more? Where do you think boar semen comes from? Do you think a boar goes into a room by himself and comes out with a sperm sample? No, farm workers collect it from him. In some instances, workers fondle their genitals and masturbate them.[221] How far from grace have we fallen that this practice exists, is common, and is laughed at when revealed?

It's no wonder that in this climate, animals on factory farms are sexually assaulted. Years ago, an undercover PETA investigation revealed a supervisor at a Hormel supplier ramming gate rods and canes into pigs' vaginas and anuses and urging his worker to expose his genitals to the pigs.[222] Hormel's response: "We find the images in the video appalling and they are inconsistent with our standards and industry standards for animal handling."[223] I'm sure it will never happen again, right?

It has been widely reported that pigs are as smart as dogs and smarter than three-year-old children, but clearly, they're treated with none of the reverence we reserve for those beings.[224] They're brutalized, just so we can eat ham, bacon, hot dogs, bologna, salami, sausage, and pork chops. Undercover investigations of factory farms are constantly revealing the most hideous and egregious abuse: workers killing pigs by slamming their heads against the floor, beating them with hammers and metal rods, and jabbing clothespins into their eyes and faces.[225] And this is before they're even taken to slaughter.

Whether they're raised on organic free-range farms or factory farms, all animals are eventually transported to slaughter. They're frightened of the transport trailers and the imminent doom, so in order to force them to move, handlers shock pigs with electric prods. Not that it would matter anyway, but there are no federal laws regulating the voltage or use of electric prods on pigs.[226] They're transported in extreme heat and cold, with little to no protection from the elements. In the summer, many die from heat exhaustion; in the winter, many arrive frozen to death, or alive, but frozen to the insides of the trucks.[227] According to a worker, "They're still alive, and they'll hook a cable on it and pull it out, maybe pull a leg off."[228]

Another worker said there were "large piles of dead hogs every day. They must've been losing fifteen to twenty out of each truckload."[229] Every year in the United States, at least one million pigs die in transport or arrive crippled from the journey.[230] One million is the number offered up by the pig industry, so it's likely a low estimate.[231] One million reasons that bacon jokes aren't funny.

MURDER 101

In case you're not familiar with how kill lines work at slaughterhouses, here's a little 101: First, the hogs are supposed to be stunned, whether by an electrical stunner, carbon dioxide gassing, or a captive bolt shot into the head.[232] Then they get shackled upside down by their leg(s). Then, they go down the line where the "sticker" stabs open their throats. Then, they're supposed to bleed to death, before being dunked into the scalding tanks. In order to help remove their coarse, bristly hair, the animals are submerged into 140°F water. This is how it's all supposed to go.

Slaughterhouses operate at crazy-fast speeds—more animals killed means more money; a typical slaughterhouse will kill more than a thousand pigs per hour.[233] Workers can't keep up. Pigs are often improperly stunned and fully conscious while having their throats stabbed. Some haven't yet bled to death when they're forced into the scalding tanks, burned alive.

Gail Eisnitz is the chief investigator for the Humane Farming Association. She traveled the country interviewing dozens of workers from different slaughterhouses, and chronicled the experience in her book *Slaughter-house*. Every single person she interviewed admitted to abusing the animals or neglecting to report those who did.[234] I read *Slaughterhouse* when researching and writing my first book, *Skinny Bitch*. It's incredibly well researched and written, and as grotesque as this might sound, a page-turner. Despite it being a difficult book to stomach, I cannot recommend it enough.

A compelling and sickening aspect of the book are the quotes of the slaughterhouse workers. One said: "These hogs get up to the scalding tank, hit the water and start screaming and kicking. Sometimes they thrash so much they kick water out of the tank. . . . Sooner or later they drown. There's a rotating arm that pushes them under, no chance for them to get out. I'm not sure if they burn to death before they drown, but it takes them a couple of minutes to stop thrashing."[235] Another, when asked about if he ever saw anyone beating hogs, said, "That's all the time." Laughing, he continued, "If the government's not around, which they're not, employees can get to beating that hog all they want to. The supervisor will not say nothing to that person. Because I have seen supervisors taking pipes and whatever they can to hit the hogs and knock them down." Asked if he ever renders them unconscious that way, he answered, "I've done it. Supervisors do it. But to do that, you got to hit them like you're hitting a baseball. You got to hit them across the head and knock them flat out."[236]

If you're American, you might be thinking, "How is this possible? What about the USDA?" According to a slaughterhouse worker, "Nobody knows who's responsible for correcting animal abuse at the plant. The USDA does zilch."[237] Mahatma Gandhi said, "The greatness of a nation and its moral progress can be judged by the way its animals are treated." Uh-oh. Not so great, America. *Not so great.*

Eisnitz chronicled the constant failure of inspectors to stop these horrors and their willingness to look the other way.[238] Think about it: In the United States alone, we kill nine billion land animals for food every single year. How could we possibly have enough inspectors on hand to supervise that volume of animals? And more relevant than that, how could we possibly raise and kill that many animals every year in a humane way? The sad truth is, we can't. If you're horrified about the way pigs are being treated and genuinely want their suffering to end, you're going to have to stop eating them.

DON'T HAVE A COW

In addition to being beautiful, cows are also extremely intelligent. Not only are they good at problem solving, but also they show excitement when they figure things out.[239] They enjoy their intelligence! It likely came as a shock to most people when *The Science Observer* revealed that cows are "capable of solving riddles with an intellect more traditionally associated with an ape."[240] Another big stir was created when *The Sunday Times (UK)* reported that cows nurture friendships and bear grudges.[241] Likely unsurprised by both reports was Susie Coston, the national shelter director for Farm Sanctuary. (Farm Sanctuary is one of my favorite nonprofits—in addition to advocacy work and educational outreach, they rescue and provide sanctuary for farm animals.) Susie tells the story of "BBFFs (Best Bovine Friends Forever)," Linda and Tricia. Linda arrived at the sanctuary with a stiff gait and twisted back legs and feet, due to a broken pelvis from calf-hood that had never been treated. Nothing could be done to help her without risking further harm, so the decision was made that she'd have to live with the goats and sheep—living with the other cows could be dangerous because they were much bigger than her and could accidentally injure her. Linda lived happily among the goats and sheep, but it was also obvious that she wanted to mix it up with the other cows, who mooed at her from a few barns away.

One day, a blind cow named Tricia arrived at the farm. She was the tiniest cow the Farm Sanctuary staff had ever seen. Naturally, she seemed like the perfect fit for Linda. Susie quickly dewormed and vaccinated Tricia, and made sure she was healthy so she could introduce her to Linda. But Tricia was inconsolably distraught—her only calf had recently been taken to slaughter. She was clearly devastated and grieving the loss of her son.

But little Tricia's heart was healed when she met Linda. She was "beside herself with joy and spent hours licking Linda over and over again." Linda was a little apprehensive at first, but within hours, she was returning the licks. The two friends have become inseparable.[242] Farm Sanctuary not only rescued each of these girls from slaughter, but also gave them the gift of love and friendship.

Sadly, most cows don't have happy endings like these two. In fact, their lives are horror shows. Males killed for their flesh are castrated, which means having their scrotums sliced open, their testicles dissected out, and the connecting cord and veins cut and the testicles removed.[243] Or, a tight rubber band get puts around the scrotum, cutting off the blood supply, so that in two to four weeks, the deadened testicles will fall off.[244] Another option: a pliers-like clamp crushes the scrotum, nerves, spermatic cord, and vessels of each testicle without breaking the skin.[245] Men, imagine having to undergo any one of these procedures with top-notch doctors at the best hospitals in the world with all the anesthesia and painkillers you want. It would still be a nightmare, right? Now imagine having to go through it at the hands of a minimum-wage ranch worker, on some dirty farm, with zero anesthetics or pain relief.

These poor souls also have their nerve-filled horns sawed or chopped off their heads.[246] If the cow is less than two months old, his horn buds will be gouged or scooped out with a knife or another sharp object, or they'll be burned off.[247] And, they have their flesh burned to the third-degree when they're being branded with irons that have been heated to 968°F.[248] Yes, this hurts; no, they aren't given painkillers.

In factory farming Concentrated Animal Feed Operations (CAFOs), the goal is to fatten beef cows in as short a time as possible. Even though they're natural herbivores, cows are given high protein grain-based feed, chicken manure, and animal by-products from slaughterhouses, including "trimmings that originate on the killing floor, inedible parts and organs, cleaned entrails, fetuses. . . ."[249] This, of course, can lead to painful, sometimes fatal, stomach problems.[250] Additionally, they're at the mercy of the elements—many die from exposure to scorching heat, freezing cold, seasonal flooding,[251] hurricanes,[252] and tornadoes.[253]

Dairy cows don't fare any better than beef cows. Like humans, cows only produce milk when they have babies. In that PETA magazine I got in the mail on that fateful day during college, there was a picture taken at a livestock auction of a dairy cow. She was lying in a puddle of mud, still alive but with her neck askew, her tongue sticking out of her mouth, and her eyes bulging out of her head. When her calf had been taken from her, she became so distressed that she started ramming herself against the stall door through which her baby had been taken. In doing so, she broke her own neck. She was left to die in that puddle of mud, with a broken neck and brokenhearted.

Like female pigs, dairy cows are subjected to constant cycles of pregnancy, labor, and delivery. This of course can begin with a worker collecting semen from males and inserting it into females. Because humans handling a bull's penis and a cow's vagina are all a totally normal part of the food chain, right? Next up for the females: having their babies taken from them. Then, their milk—which was meant for their kidnapped babies—is extracted from their bodies. And in this age of industrialized farming, this means several times a day electronic milking machines are attached to their udders. Like humans, cows' bodies naturally produce just enough milk for their calves. But on factory farms, more milk means more money. Because of selective breeding; high-protein feed; mechanized milking; and the administering of growth hormones, dairy production today is ten times what nature intended.[254] The constant cycle of pregnancy and milk production is taxing on these poor childless mothers. Their natural lifespans can be up to twenty-five years, but stress, disease, lameness, and reproductive problems can render cows worthless to the dairy industry by the time they are four or five.[255]

So what happens to their babies? Mercy for Animals, one of my favorite nonprofits, recently obtained undercover footage from a farm that breeds calves for dairies. Workers were recorded hitting baby cows in their skulls with pickaxes and hammers, kicking *downed* calves in the head, and standing on their necks and ribs.[256] (Downed animals are those who are too sick or too injured to walk.) Beaten calves, still alive and conscious, were haplessly thrown onto dead piles, and sick, injured, and dying calves were denied medical care.[257] I can live without cheese, but I *can't* live with contributing to any of that.

Human mothers, can you remember how you felt when you gave birth?

Can you even begin to imagine how it would feel to have your baby snatched away and your sore, sensitive breasts—producing more than ten times as much milk as nature intended—being pumped and pulled by a machine? Now imagine that your newborn daughter was to be in a life of dairy-producing servitude and your son taken away, only to be killed after three to eighteen weeks for veal.[258] Veal, a product that many consumers rightly refuse to buy due to its inherent cruelty, is a direct by-product of the dairy industry. Milk and cheese habits beget veal.

Clearly, at the hands of humans, life for dairy cows, beef cows, and veal calves is not good. And neither is death. These animals do not want to be taken on a death march anymore than you or I would. When they get loaded onto and offloaded from trucks, they are stressed and afraid, some even frozen with fear. And many others are too sick or injured to walk. So workers employ any means necessary to get the cows moving. According to a former USDA inspector, "Uncooperative animals are beaten, they have prods poked in their faces and up their rectums."[259] Cows are dragged with chains, shocked continuously, yanked by their tails—whatever it takes. A slaughterhouse worker said, "I've drug cows till their bones start breaking, while they were still alive. Bringing them around the corner and they get stuck up in the doorway, just pull them till their hide be ripped, till the blood just drip on the steel and concrete. Breaking their legs. . . . And the cow be crying with its tongue stuck out. They pull him till his neck just pop."[260]

I travel a lot. And even on short road trips in comfortable cars—with lots of water and snacks and pee breaks—I get a little tweaked. Cows can spend up to twenty-eight consecutive hours (thirty-six if a written request is submitted) packed into a truck with no food, water, or breaks, and no protection from sun, heat, cold, rain, or snow.[261] Vomit, urine, feces, and diarrhea are part of the equation, and of course, they just have to stand in it, or, if they're unable to stand, lie in it. Cows who are dead on arrival are also a constant variable. Maybe they're the lucky ones, since others can literally have body parts frozen to the floor or sides of the truck.[262] And this is just the transportation part.

Now for the slaughter part: Cows are shot in the head with a captive bolt, shackled and hung upside down, stabbed in the throats, skinned, and eviscerated. They're supposed to be unconscious for the throat stabbing, but they can be totally awake and aware and bellowing in pain and terror. Worse, they're sometimes fully conscious when they reach the "skinners," which means they're being skinned alive.[263] Worse still, some are still conscious after being skinned, while being hacked apart. According to a *Washington Post* exposé, "Some would survive as far as the tail cutter, the belly ripper, and the hide puller. 'They die piece by piece.'"[264]

BIRDS OF A FEATHER GET TORTURED TOGETHER

When I ate "chicken" or "turkey," it never dawned on me that I was eating *a chicken* or *a turkey*. Piece by piece. Asking for a drumstick meant a specific meat cut; it never occurred to me that it was the *leg* of a *bird* who had once been alive. I think it's a common disconnect for people, which would explain why, worldwide, we casually and thoughtlessly kill fifty billion chickens every year.[265]

Like factory-farmed cows and pigs, birds are also subject to sexual abuse and human perversion. A PETA undercover investigator said he saw a worker for a Butterball supplier simulate raping a turkey whose head and legs were restrained in metal shackles.[266] Another worker was seen jamming his finger into a bird's vagina while it hung on the slaughter line.[267] Butterball responded saying they take "any allegations of animal mistreatment very seriously" and that they have "a zero tolerance policy for animal abuse."[268] I'll let you decide whether you believe that. Male turkeys are restrained and masturbated for semen collection; females are restrained and inseminated.[269] Breeding has made them larger than nature intended so turkeys can't even mate normally.[270] One hundred percent of commercially raised turkeys in the United States are produced using artificial insemination.[271] *Happy Thanksgiving, here's a cornucopia of bestiality and rape.*

Years ago, I went to Farm Sanctuary in Orland, California. I loved meeting all the animals, but it was the birds who stole the show. The turkeys bum-rushed me, hunkered down at my feet, and waited to get pet. They were just like dogs. They couldn't get enough love or affection. My friend Gretchen sometimes volunteers at Animal Acres, another paradise for rescued animals. Some of the braver chickens would either sit on her shoulder or on her lap, cooing with pleasure at being held and pet. They'd also run full tilt when a special food treat was brought out for them. These birds are not only funny and sweet, but also smart. Their cognitive capacities have been said to be equivalent to primates.[272] And yet . . .

"Broiler" chickens are raised and killed for their flesh. "Breeders" are chickens who are used to produce broiler chickens. And "egg-laying" hens are those exploited so we can eat their eggs. They all suffer miserably on factory farms and in slaughterhouses.

"BROILERS"

Anyone who's particularly maternal is often referred to as a "mother hen." And for good reason: chickens are protective, nurturing parents. So much so that there are countless stories of them "adopting" bunnies, kittens, and even whole litters of puppies.[273] Yet despite their natural affinity for parenting, they never get to raise their babies on factory farms. Broiler chickens are killed when they're only six weeks old.[274] They can spend their entire short lives packed into excrement-filled sheds with tens of thousands of other birds, many suffering from gastrointestinal and blood diseases, respiratory illnesses, and blinding eye maladies (like ammonia burn) from the filthy living conditions.[275] When Michael Specter, a journalist for the New Yorker, went inside a chicken shed, he wrote, "I was almost knocked to the ground by the overpowering smell of feces and ammonia. My eyes burned and so did my lungs, and I could neither see nor breathe. . . . There must have been 30,000 chickens sitting silently on the floor in front of me. They didn't move, didn't cluck. They were almost like statues of chickens, living in nearly total darkness, and they would spend every minute of their six-week lives that way."[276]

Perhaps the chickens weren't moving because they couldn't. Due to genetic manipulation and the administration of growth-promoting antibiotics, by the age of six weeks, 90 percent of broilers are so obese they can't even walk normally.[277] The average breast size of a broiler chicken is seven times heavier today than it was twenty-five years ago; many of these poor babies die from heart attacks, lung collapse,[278] and organ failure.[279] And because their bodies are so much larger than what nature intended, crippling leg deformities are common.[280] So many of these poor broken birds die when they can no longer reach the water nozzles.[281]

"BREEDERS"

....

The parents of these broilers are "breeder" chickens, and they too are denied access to sunlight, fresh air, or anything else they would normally enjoy in nature. Common industry practice dictates that when they're between one and ten days old,[282] one-half to two-thirds of their beaks[283] are seared off their faces with a hot blade, so that they won't peck each other due to the stresses of living in such severe confinement.[284] Debeaking. Of course, they aren't given any painkillers. Some of the birds die on the spot from shock, others starve to death because they're in such excruciating pain, they can't eat.[285] Sometimes their toes, spurs, and combs are cut off, too.[286]

Chickens in the wild can live from seven to fifteen years; breeders are killed when they're about a year old.[287] While this is a short amount of time compared to their natural lifespan, it's a long time to live in a body that's been selectively bred and genetically engineered for rapid growth. Their legs are horribly crippled and deformed, and the likelihood of organ failure and fatality is even higher in these miserable birds than in broilers.[288] In a pitiful attempt to combat these problems, many factory-farm operators will severely limit the amount of food given to them.[289] Some will even stick plastic rods up the tiny, sensitive nasal cavities of the male birds. These rods stick out on both sides of the birds' faces and keep them from being able to reach through the barrier to the females' food.[290] So now, on top of being mutilated, crippled, injured, and confined, these birds (both male and female) are also painfully hungry and agitated.[291] When they drink more water to stave off the hunger, industry protocol proffers reducing their drinking water so farm operators don't have to deal with wet manure.[292] After a year of this hellish existence, when their bodies are too broken and depleted to breed anymore, they are sent to slaughter.

KILLING BROILERS AND BREEDERS

Even though chickens make up 98 percent of the land animals we kill in the United States, birds are excluded from the Humane Slaughter Act.[293] Who suggested this? Who agreed to this? How did they get away with this? How do they still get away with this? We kill 100 times more chickens than pigs and 250 times more chickens than cows, yet there are no federal laws mandating that chickens be rendered unconscious before slaughter.[294] Please be appropriately appalled.

Broilers and breeders go through traditional kill lines, much like cows and pigs. They're shackled upside down by a leg, for starters. However, when chickens struggle, it's more likely that the mechanized throat slasher will miss its mark. So chickens are dragged upside down through an electrically charged water bath. This paralyzes them, but doesn't necessarily render them unconscious or desensitized to pain.[295] So not only do they feel the electrified bath, but they also feel the slash of the blade. Who suggested this? Who agreed to this? How did they get away with this? How do they still get away with this? Sometimes the blade catches a throat, sometimes it gets them in another area of the body, and sometimes it misses altogether. Next up is the scalding tank, to remove the birds' feathers. Because of the speed of the kill line and its imperfections, like pigs, chickens are often submerged into scalding tanks fully conscious, where they "scream, kick, and their eyeballs pop out of their heads."[296] I assume you're appropriately appalled.

EGGS AREN'T ALL THEY'RE
CRACKED UP TO BE

Most egg-laying hens are put out of their misery when they are between one and two years old. But before then, not only are they subjected to debeaking, but they're also crammed into cages with, on average, about four or five other birds.[297] The hens are so crowded in the cages they can't stretch their wings and can barely turn around.[298] Each bird is allotted less space than a standard piece of paper.[299] The cages are stacked on top of each other, filling sheds with up to 125,000 birds[300]—and in some cases, many more.[301] They can hardly move, let alone groom or take care of themselves. The only option they have is whether to stand or slump on the hard wire floor—standing means causing painful sores on the feet, slumping means painful sores on the body.[302] In natural habitats, they'd be able to scratch their claws, which would keep them a healthy length. On factory farms, their claws grow painfully and unnaturally long.[303]

In the wild, chickens will go through a molting process over two to four months where they'll shed old feathers and grow new ones, and recharge and rejuvenate their bodies. After molting, their rested bodies will have replenished lost nutrients from previous egg-laying, and they'll be ready to lay more eggs. In order for factory-farm operators to maximize their profits, many try to maximize egg production through "forced molting." By either feeding chickens nutrient deficient fillers,[304] severely restricting their rations, or starving them completely for one to three weeks straight,[305] egg producers shock the hens' bodies into additional egg-laying cycles. This of course, takes a toll on the birds, who often tear out the feathers of their cagemates and try to digest them; many die.[306]

In general, egg production can be taxing for chickens, who lose a lot of calcium in the process. Because they're forced to lay more eggs than what's natural and are unable to exercise due to confinement, many farmed hens develop osteoporosis. This depletion of minerals and breaking of bones can kill many chickens, leaving them dying in their cages, often with their heads trapped between bars.[307] Constantly having to lay eggs, day in and day out, other hens suffer slow, agonizing deaths from uterine prolapse—when their uteruses get pushed out of their vents.[308] Women, imagine for someone's financial gain, having to give birth over and over again, to the extent that your uterus comes out of your vagina. And you don't get any medical treatment, or even a quiet, comfortable bed to suffer in. You and your infected, exposed organ are stuffed into an excrement-filled jail cell with a bunch of other women just like you. This is the life of an egg-laying hen. The ones who don't die in these horrific ways are shipped off to slaughter. But their bodies are so worn, they'll be turned into dog food, cat food, or farm animal feed because their flesh is too bruised and battered to be much else.[309]

THE LAST STOP

Sadly, bruising and battering is also part of the transportation and slaughter process for broilers and breeders. As usual, time is money. "Catchers" grab birds from their cages by their leg(s), two to four birds in each hand, upside down, and throw or stuff them into transport crates. The terrified animals are of course struggling, flapping, and crying out.[310] Once they arrive at their destination, they have to be unloaded from the trucks and crates, so it happens all over again. You'd never know they were transporting living beings; they might as well be tossing around fake rubber chickens. Many animals are injured. Egg-laying hens, whose poor bodies have been so depleted of calcium, are especially susceptible to bone breaks.[311] But all the birds are fragile, and none are spared the roughness or insensitivity of the workers. Each year during transport alone, hundreds of millions of chickens will suffer broken legs and wings, lacerations, hemorrhage, dehydration, heat exhaustion, hypothermia, and heart failure.[312] Millions die.[313]

TAKING OUT THE TRASH

Every year, worldwide, six billion newly hatched chicks are killed[314]—not to be eaten as meat, not to be made into soup, and not for dog or cat food. These one- or two-day-old babies are killed just because they're males, which means they're useless to egg producers. Because of selective breeding, they'll never be "meaty" enough to sell for their flesh, and because they're male, they'll never lay eggs. So on factory farms, they amount to trash that needs to be disposed of. Literally. In some cases, these newborn babies are heaped into garbage bags and thrown into dumpsters . . . alive. They're simply left to die, either by suffocation, starvation, dehydration, or exposure. Or when a worker stomps on the "trash" to make room for more "trash," they'll be killed.[315] In other cases, these little peeps are thrown into a macerator, a large high-speed grinder.[316] They're ground up and liquified like they aren't living, feeling beings, but just lumps of play-dough going through a play-dough machine. I know with such a long litany of horrors, it might be easy to check out or disconnect. But this is real, this is happening, and you need to know. So try to hang in there if your brain is slipping.

ORGANIC SHMORGANIC

···

When I first learned about the horrors of egg production, I stopped buying conventionally produced eggs and bought organic, free-range eggs instead. What I didn't know at the time (and it's the same now) was that a lot of free-range claims are bogus, and that "free" could just mean that one door is left open for five minutes and that only thirty of 30,000 chickens can get through.[317] And that "range" can mean a cement-covered patch between two ramshackle sheds.[318] Certainly cage-free is better than caged, but it's only the lesser of two evils. Neither are cruelty-free. The other factor I didn't take into account was that even if the chickens (or cows or pigs) did come from an organic farm, a family farm, or a free-range farm, many still had to endure the transportation process and all of them were ultimately killed.

"Humane slaughter" is a laughable oxymoron. There's a perfect example—video footage taken from a small, free-range farm, where just a small group of chickens are killed as "humanely" as possible. Google "Free range chicken slaughter video" and judge for yourself whether this looks humane. According to Woodstock Farm Animal Sanctuary, another awesome nonprofit: "If you're buying 'cage free,' 'free range,' or 'humane certified' eggs from a grocery store, you are more than likely being deceived about the welfare of egg-laying hens. Because 'humane' labeling terms are not meaningfully defined or enforced, suppliers are notorious for manipulating intentional loopholes in these loosely interpreted standards."[319]

PER-POO

The only thing more disgusting than mistreating animals is mistreating animals, pretending you're not, getting the public thinking that humane treatment is a priority for your company, and advertising your products under that guise. The USDA has implemented something called the Process Verified Program, which allows companies to do just that. There are thirteen companies on the Official Listing of Approved USDA Process Verified Programs for poultry. Twelve of them are Perdue (for Perdue and Harvestland brands). At the bottom of the list is a footnote saying, "Humanely Raised Program claim is in accordance with Perdue's Best Practices."[320] Oh, I see. Perdue gets to dictate what's humane, and then the USDA affirms it with a seal of approval.

Thankfully, in 2010, the Humane Society of the United States (HSUS) filed a class-action lawsuit against Perdue, alleging that "humanely raised" labeling claims violate the Consumer Fraud Act. Perdue responded with a statement saying that its farmers' handling of their chickens "is exceeding the industry standards."[321] They claimed the Humane Society's suit was based on "narrow, arbitrary standards" of humane treatment.[322] *Yeah, I believe you Perdue. Sure.* Jonathan Lovvorn, a senior vice president and chief counsel of Animal Protection Litigation for HSUS, said "Companies like Perdue are exploiting the dramatic growth of consumer demand for improved animal welfare for their own profit. Rather than implementing humane reforms, Perdue has simply slapped 'humanely raised' stickers on its factory-farmed products, hoping consumers won't know the difference."[323]

Perdue isn't the only one allegedly "exploiting consumer demand for improved animal welfare." In November of 2011, ABC's *Good Morning America*, *World News Tonight*, and *20/20* aired undercover video footage shot by a

Mercy for Animals investigator. It was filmed over nine weeks in eight separate facilities of Sparboe Farms, one of America's largest egg suppliers.[324] The footage shows birds crammed into small battery cages; decomposing dead birds left in cages with live birds; painful debeaking (burning the beaks off chicks without any anesthetics); sadistic and malicious abuse; and the "disposing of" male chicks—throwing them away, as garbage, into trash bags.[325] Sparboe Farms was sporting the "humanely raised" seal on their packaging—they had been approved, audited, and certified by the USDA through its Process Verified Program.[326] Fascinating/despicable. (Sparboe told ABC news that the undercover film was an aberration and that the company had zero tolerance for abuse of animals. *Uh huh, of course.*)

ACTS OF GOD

By the way, all these terrible things that happen are inherent in the mass production of animals for food. And they don't even take into account accidents or acts of God. What happens to animals when earthquakes, hurricanes, tornadoes, and floods hit? Like animals in zoos, factory-farmed animals are confined and have no chance of escape. They're left to die; there are no massive evacuation plans for farm animals. And when transport trucks crash or overturn, animals languish for hours in the freezing cold or sweltering heat in mangled cages with untreated injuries. For our dogs, we pray that they die in their sleep. For our dinners, we contribute to living hell for cows, chickens, and pigs. In the words of Ralph Waldo Emerson: "You have just dined, and however scrupulously the slaughterhouse is concealed in the graceful distance of miles, there is complicity."

FISH OUT OF WATER

....

The first year I stopped eating animals, I still ate fish. As bad as I felt for cows, chickens, and pigs, I simply didn't consider that fish *felt*. So I ate them, and contributed to the annual death toll of ninety billion marine animals.[327] But science has proven time and time and time again that fish do feel pain, just like every other animal. They also experience fear. Research has also shown that fish make distress sounds, and that they grunt when in fear.[328] They even grunt with *anticipatory* fear.[329] Fish communicate with each other through squeaks, squeals, and other low-frequency sounds; some sing to woo mating partners; and one study revealed their ability to press food-dispensing levers at specific times—fish can tell time![330] (They also have long-term memories,[331] so cramming them into fishbowls and aquariums isn't a good environment for them.)

Fish and Fisheries, a scientific journal, cites more than 500 research papers on fish intelligence, affirming that fish are smart, socially intelligent, cooperative, able to use tools, and that they have sophisticated social structures and impressive long-term memories.[332] One type of rainbow fish learned to escape from a net in their tank . . . they then demonstrated that they remembered how they did it eleven months later![333] Scientists compare this to a human recalling a lesson learned forty years earlier.[334] Incredibly, a biologist studying the evolution of cognition in fish, says, "In many areas, such as memory, their cognitive powers match or exceed those of 'higher' vertebrates, including nonhuman primates."[335] As smart as or smarter than primates! An Oxford scientist states that fish are "very capable of learning and remembering, and possess a range of cognitive skills that would surprise many people."[336]

I'll be the first to admit that I was surprised. I had never thought of fish as smart. I just felt sorry for any living being that got hooked in the face. Too bad all the methods for catching fish equate to massive suffering.

THERE'S MORE THAN ONE
WAY TO KILL A FISH

Bottom trawlers are catastrophic for marine life and for the ocean itself. Humongous bag-shaped nets are dragged along the ocean floor, catching everything in their paths. Not only do target fish get netted (like orange roughy, haddock, and cod), but so do rocks and coral and nontarget animals (also known as bycatch). The force of the net and all the debris in it can completely ground the scales off the trapped fish or crush them to death.[337] When hoisted out of the water, the decompression ruptures their swim bladders, pops out their eyes, and pushes their esophagi and stomachs out through their mouths.[338] Bottom trawling scrapes all signs of life off the ocean floor; no wonder it's considered the underwater equivalent of clear-cutting forests.[339] Shrimp trawling is notorious for being the worst offender, with nontarget species making up more than 80 percent of the catch.[340] Meaning: 80 percent of what gets caught gets thrown back into the water like garbage, dead or dying.

The primary method to catch tuna is the use of a purse seine (which is also used to catch other species). Fishermen track dolphins, who swim with large tuna, and then drop a net into the water to surround the tuna. They then cinch the edges of the net together, trapping the fish. (Yes, dolphins can get caught in the nets, too.) Remember, we now know that fish are smart and that they experience fear. These fish must be so scared, gasping for breath as they're pulled out of the water. If they haven't died from decompression or suffocation by the time they reach the boat deck, they can still be conscious when their gills are slit and they're disemboweled.[341]

Gill nets, which are weighted at the bottom and held upright by floats at the top can be over a mile·long. These "walls of death" trap fish who can't see the netting, and swim right into them. If they try to back out, their gills and fins get caught. If they can't swim, they can't breathe, and they suffocate to death. Or, in their panic to free themselves, they cut their struggling bodies on the sharp mesh and bleed to death. Gill nets are left unmonitored for days at a time and are totally indiscriminate, which of course means lots of bycatch. Whales, dolphins, and porpoises—including at-risk species—are killed in droves.[342] Remember from earlier in the chapter, those 30,000 whales and dolphins who are being purposely hunted and killed annually that we're all so furious about—it's estimated that 300,000 whales, dolphins, and porpoises are killed by fishing gear every year.[343]

Some of those 300,000 are also killed by longline fishing, which is one of the most widespread fishing practices. Up to seventy-five miles of line are unspooled behind ships—floating at the surface or weighted at different depths—and on these lines are thousands of baited hooks. Unsuspecting animals—including fish, sharks, sea turtles, marine birds, whales, dolphins, porpoises, seals, and sea lions—can all fall prey. A hook in the face is bad enough, but some animals drown, others bleed to death, and others struggle for hours until they get reeled in. Many of these nontarget animals will simply be tossed back into the water, dead or injured. Hundreds of millions of fish and other marine animals are incidentally killed every year as bycatch. Big target fish, like swordfish and yellowfin tuna, get dragged toward the boat, hook in face. Once they're within reach of the boat, fishermen will sink pickaxes into whatever part of the fish they can, so long as it allows them to haul them into the boat.[344]

In addition to being totally cruel, the fishing industry has completely jacked up our ocean ecosystems. In the past fifty years, 90 percent of large fish populations have been wiped out.[345] We can live without sushi, but we can't live without the oceans. Get an avocado roll.

PART II: A WHOLE DIFFERENT ANIMAL

APPLES TO ORANGES

All animals have unique personalities, the desire to live, and the ability to experience pain. I constantly hear people saying humans are "superior" to other animals, which always baffles me. Yeah, we're better at being humans and doing human stuff than they are. Agreed. But that doesn't make us smarter—it just makes us human. Would we say that sharks are superior to lions because they can swim? Or that kangaroos are superior to horses because they can jump higher? It's absurd. So what if we can build airplanes and use computers? What use does a zebra have for either? Cows are only stupid if we're measuring them by human intelligence. No, they don't speak human. And when I was in Paris, I didn't speak French. It doesn't mean I'm stupid; it just means I communicate in a different language. Perhaps if we took the time to learn the languages of these animals— instead of assuming moral superiority that they don't speak ours—we would see their intelligence and sensitivity. Animals have figured out how to live in harmony with each other and the planet. We're the only species that has completely messed up the earth—air pollution, water pollution, land degradation, rainforest destruction, ocean decimation, and climate change. We're the ones suffering from addiction to alcohol, food, drugs, tobacco, work, TV, sex, pornography, cell phones; we're the ones depressed, anxious, angry, and lethargic; we're the ones who seem to have it all, yet can't make our lives work. Our so-called complexities and intelligence haven't done us any good. It's my opinion that animals are much smarter than humans. But their intelligence is irrelevant. The systematic confinement, exploitation, and murder of living, feeling beings is wrong. Jeremy Bentham, an eighteenth-century English philosopher and social reformer hit the nail on the head when he said, about all animals, "The question is not, *Can they reason?* nor, *Can they talk?* but, *Can they suffer?*"

According to a survey of nearly 2,000 people, 92 percent agreed that it's important that farm animals are well-cared for; 85 percent said that the quality of life for farm animals is important, even when they're used for meat; 81 percent agreed that the well-being of farm animals is as important as the well-being of pets; and 75 percent agreed that farm animals should be protected from feeling physical pain.[346] Fantastic—at least three-fourths of us agree on paper that animals should be spared from suffering. Can we put that compassion into action and make different choices? Because unfortunately, sympathy alone doesn't help animals.

TO YOUR HEALTH

··

Hippocrates, the father of modern medicine, was way ahead of his time when he said: "Let food be thy medicine and medicine be thy food." But in all his wisdom, he couldn't have possibly foreseen the catastrophe we've created for ourselves. For people living in First World countries, the top killers are heart disease, stroke, cancer, and diabetes. The consumption of animal products is implicated in all of these. Maybe to protect her precious animals, Mother Nature—in her infinite wisdom—made meat, eggs, and dairy high in fat, saturated fat, and cholesterol and devoid of fiber, phytochemicals, and antioxidants. *You're gonna kill them? I'm gonna kill you. Suckas!*

In the United States, heart disease has been the number one cause of death for the past one hundred years.[347] While cancer rates are certainly high, women's death rate from heart disease is *eight times higher* than from breast cancer.[348] The Framingham Heart Study is the most well known of its kind ever conducted and definitively concluded that cholesterol has an effect on heart disease.[349] The only foods that contain cholesterol are animal foods—flesh, eggs, and dairy. Cholesterol can be lowered—reducing the risk of heart disease—by avoiding animal products.[350] Mother Nature is so clever: another way to lower cholesterol is by eating plant protein.[351] It's no wonder she made fruits and veggies so colorful and pretty and visually appealing. Savvy gal.

The most common type of heart disease is coronary artery disease, which is when the arteries to the heart are narrowed or hardened by a buildup of plaque, which can lead to heart attack. Similarly, the blood vessels to our brain are affected, which can cause cognitive impairment, dementia, Alzheimer's, and stroke.[352] Scientists did a study with 5,000 older people and found that those who consumed the most fat and saturated fat had the highest risk of dementia due to vascular problems.[353]

Diabetics have two to four times the risk of stroke and are two to four times more likely to die from heart disease.[354] Diabetes is also the leading cause of blindness in adults.[355] And while yes, sugar plays a part in the lives of diabetics, the lesser-known but more insidious bad guy is animal protein. Seventy years ago, all the existing research on diet and diabetes rates from six countries was compiled into one report.[356] Even back then, the findings were clear, and they were reaffirmed thirty years later by different researchers: Diabetes rates were lower in countries where the populations ate *less* animal protein, fat, and animal fat, and *more* plant carbohydrates.[357]

In the West, hardly any of us is untouched by cancer; we've all lost someone to this wretched disease. In the United States, we've waged a War on Cancer that's lasted more than forty years and cost hundreds of billions of dollars. Is it possible that something as simple as changing our diets could end this war, once and for all? Two studies of more than 120,000 people spanning twenty-six years found that eating red meat greatly increased the likelihood of cancer mortality.[358] The more meat consumed, the higher the risk.[359] And if the participants were eating processed meat, like bacon, the risk was even higher.[360] According to a major Harvard study of 135,000 people, those who frequently ate grilled, skinless chicken (which is supposed to be the "healthiest" kind) had a fifty-two percent higher chance of developing bladder cancer than those who didn't.[361] The World Health Organization analyzed data from thirty-four countries and correlated egg consumption with mortality from colon and rectal cancers.[362] Another study revealed that even moderate egg consumption tripled the risk of bladder cancer.[363]

In addition to being high in cholesterol, fish flesh (including shellfish) can also accumulate extremely high levels of carcinogenic chemical residues, like polychlorinated biphenyls (PCBs).[364] Our waterways are polluted with countless industrial pollutants, and these toxins get absorbed into the flesh of the fish. Farm-raised fish aren't any better: farmed salmon has seven times more PCBs than wild-caught salmon.[365]

A review of twenty-three studies revealed, " . . . animal protein, meats, dairy products and eggs have frequently been associated with a higher risk of prostate cancer . . . "[366]

According to two major Harvard studies, men who drink milk have a thirty to sixty percent greater risk of prostate cancer than those who avoid dairy.[367] Prostate cancer is the most commonly diagnosed cancer in American men.[368] And one of the most consistent, specific links between diet and prostate cancer is dairy.[369]

Does breast cancer run in your family? One research group found that less than 3 percent of breast cancers are related to family history.[370] But casein (milk protein) has been linked to all three stages of cancer: initiation, growth, and promotion.[371]

And in case you still think you need dairy for strong bones, the Harvard Nurses' Health Study followed more than 72,000 women over the course of twelve years—increased milk consumption was *not shown* to have a protective effect on bones.[372] Researchers at Yale did a study using thirty-four surveys from sixteen countries found in twenty-nine research publications. They reported the same findings.[373] Americans are among the top consumers of dairy products in the world. So if dairy does what the dairy industry claims, we should have among the lowest rates of osteoporosis in the world, right? According to the *Journal of Gerontology*, American women over fifty have among the highest rates of hip fractures in the world. The only countries with higher rates are those that consume more milk.[374]

The decades-long research is evident: People who ate the most animal foods got the most chronic diseases; people who ate the most plant foods were the healthiest.[375] (Even small intakes of animal products were associated with negative effects.)[376]

THE GROSS FACTOR

Are you getting the picture? Animal products *aren't healthy for human consumption.* And that's even before we start messing with animals, breeding them by the billions. As revealed by two-time Pulitzer Prize–winner and *New York Times* columnist Nicholas Kristof, two scientific studies suggested factory-farmed chickens are fed:[377]

- caffeine to keep them awake and eating

- active ingredients of Tylenol and Benadryl to reduce anxiety (which can affect meat toughness and growth rate)

- arsenic

- banned antibiotics

Legal antibiotics are also administered, not only to help ward off disease—since they're living in filthy, confined quarters with tens of thousands other animals—but also to help them grow bigger and faster.[378] A USDA study of flies and cockroaches from pig farm manure found that the bugs carried the same antibiotic-resistant bacteria as the pigs.[379] It's been widely believed that feeding antibiotics to animals is causing antibiotic-resistance to superbugs in humans who eat their flesh, eggs, and dairy. (Of course, the farming industry denies these accusations.) But if we're sick and need meds that work, we may be out of luck. Maybe that sounds like no big whoop, but antibiotic-resistant infections kill more people every year than AIDS.[380] A whopping 80 percent of all antibiotics sold in the United States are given to livestock.[381]

According to a former poultry plant worker from the '80s, poultry plants sound like the grossest places on earth. She said there were flies, rats, and five-inch-long flying cockroaches covering the walls and floors.[382] Wait, it gets worse: "After they are hung, sometimes the chickens fall off into the drain that runs down the middle of the line. This is where roaches, intestines, diseased parts, fecal contamination, and blood are washed down. Workers [vomit] into the drain. . . . Employees are constantly chewing and spitting out snuff and tobacco on the floor . . . sometimes they have to relieve themselves on the floor . . . supervisors told us to take the fallen chickens out of the drain and send them down the line."[383] A USDA inspector said of the cockroaches, "One time we shined a flashlight into a hole they were crawling in and out, and they were so thick it was like maggots, you couldn't even see the surface."[384] A worker at another poultry plant said, "Every day, I saw black chicken, green chicken, chicken that stank, and chicken with feces on it. Chicken like this is supposed to be thrown away, but instead it would be sent down the line to be processed."[385] Another worker at another plant said, "I personally have seen rotten meat—you can tell by the odor. This rotten meat is mixed with the fresh meat and sold for baby food. We are asked to mix it with the fresh food, and this is the way it is sold. You can see the worms inside the meat."[386] *Consumer Reports* did a study in 2006 of grocery-store-bought chickens. A staggering 83 percent tested were infected with either campylobacter, salmonella, or both.[387] Not so surprising.

"WHERE DO YOU GET YOUR PROTEIN?"

Why are we eating this stuff if it's unhealthy and totally nasty? We've been conditioned and brainwashed into thinking we need to. Everyone and their mother thinks you need to eat animal products for protein; too bad everyone and their mother has been misinformed. According to *The China Study*'s Dr. T. Colin Campbell, our protein intake only needs to be about 5 to 6 percent of our total caloric intake.[388] Dr. Campbell got his PhD from Cornell, has authored over 300 research papers, and has *four decades* of high-level research experience. *The China Study* is the most comprehensive study of diet and nutrition ever conducted in history—spanning over twenty years time; citing from more than 750 references; and partnering Cornell University, Oxford University, and the Chinese Academy of Preventative Medicine. I trust Dr. Campbell. I don't trust the government, whose recommended daily allowance of protein is 10 to 35 percent. You can decide for yourself whether to trust the government or Dr. Campbell. But know that Dr. Campbell says that "diets with more animal-based protein will create higher blood cholesterol levels and higher risks of atherosclerosis [disease of the arteries], cancer, osteoporosis, Alzheimer's disease, and kidney stones, to name just a few chronic diseases that the FNB [Food and

Nutrition Board] chooses to ignore."[389] Dr. Campbell isn't just opposed to animal protein, he's *for* plant protein.

PLANTS RULE

To debunk another long-standing myth, vegetarians not only get enough protein, they also get enough iron. Campbell says, "People who consume more plant-based foods, thus more dietary fiber, also consume more iron, all of which results in statistically significant higher levels of hemoglobin."[390] Also, fiber and antioxidants, which we get by eating plants, are linked to lower risks of breast cancer and cancers of the digestive tracts.[391]

Nature is nothing short of miraculous. While the sun, industrial pollutants, and bad diets can cause free radical damage (which can lead to cancer), fruits grow on trees, we eat them, and we fight cancer. As reported in *The China Study*, cancer rates were five to eight times higher in areas where fruit intake was lowest.[392] Plants make free-radical shields; humans don't. But Nature makes plants pretty and appealing; we eat them; and we get shielded.[393]

Plant foods aren't just for tree huggers, though. They're for everyone, even growing children and those who want to muscle up. Body growth is linked to protein in general, not just animal protein.[394] So we can feed our kids and our bodybuilders plant protein, watch them grow—all while not putting anything in their bodies that will increase the likelihood of cancer, heart disease, stroke, and diabetes. "Individuals can achieve their genetic potential for growth and body size by consuming a plant-based diet," says Dr. Campbell.[395] Call me a hippie, a flower child, or tree hugger, I don't care—I think Nature is friggin' amazing. And I think Dr. Campbell, one of the top scientists in the world, agrees. He's certainly clear in his declaration that "Fruits, veggies, and whole grains are the healthiest foods you can consume. . . ."[396]

PART III: LET'S DO THIS!

OUT OF THE CLOSET

For those of you who are slow on the take, I guess now would be a good time to out myself: I'm vegan. I don't eat any animals. I don't eat eggs. And I don't consume dairy products. I eat everything else. And because of the day and age we live in and all the amazing food that exists, I still get to eat pizza, cheeseburgers, french fries, cupcakes, and ice cream—all vegan. And I also get to have a reduced risk of a bunch of nasty diseases. But most important to me is that I don't participate in the confinement, torture, and slaughter of animals. Going vegetarian and then vegan were the two best decisions I've ever made. My life is completely different as a result, and all my vegan friends feel the same way.

Along with the rest of the vegan tribe, I invite you to get on the bus. We want you; we welcome you; we love you. And we know you'll love it here as much as we do. It's not an exclusive, elitist club—anyone can join, all are welcome. We want our numbers to grow. We want animals spared; we want humans to live longer, happier, healthier lives; and we want public demand for vegan food to continue growing at breakneck speeds. We also care about our planet.

INCONVENIENT TRUTHS

Animal agriculture is the number one cause of climate change.[397] Number one. It beats out all transportation in the world *combined*. By *40 percent*.[398] It's also the number one polluter of American waterways and the primary contributor of land degradation, ocean decimation, desertification, and deforestation.[399]

Another problem inherent in raising animals to feed humans is the vast amount of resources it takes. We're using up precious land, water, energy, and fuel to grow crops, turn the crops into feed, and then transport the feed to animals. And then more resources are used to process, package, and transport eggs, meat, and dairy. Growing all food is resource-intensive—just to grow one orange, it takes about thirteen gallons of water.[400] But as we add animals to the equation, it becomes much costlier. One pound of chicken requires 468 gallons of water, a gallon of milk takes 880 gallons, and a pound of beef uses 1799 gallons of water![401] There's no way around it: Real environmentalists are vegan.

Not only is meat production environmentally devastating, it's also devastating to humanity. The food we grow to feed farm animals could instead be used to feed the world's hungry. None of us needs meat to live; we eat it because we like how it tastes. If we gave up this addiction and got over that base desire, we could have enough food to feed the world's hungry. Instead, we all tsk and say what a shame it is that people are starving all over the world.

Not only are starving humans affected by the meat industry, so are the people working in it. Human Rights Watch (HRW) is one of the world's leading independent nonprofits dedicated to defending and protecting human rights. They regularly and systematically conduct investigations of human rights violations in seventy countries. In 2005, for the first time since their formation thirty years ago, they criticized a U.S. industry.[402] Their eighteen-page report is called "Blood, Sweat, and Fear: Workers' Rights in U.S. Meat and Poultry Plants." It details the constant risk, fear, danger, and difficulties faced by workers in beef, pork, and poultry slaughtering and processing plants.[403] HRW revealed that meatpacking and slaughterhouse employers:

- expose workers to severe, life-threatening, and sometimes fatal injuries that are predictable and preventable

- "frustrate" workers' efforts to get compensation for injuries sustained while on the job

- "crush" workers' self-organizing efforts and rights of association[404]

HRW is careful to point out that, "These are not occasional lapses by employers paying insufficient attention to modern human resources management policies. These are systematic human rights violations embedded in meat and poultry industry employment."[405] While all workers are susceptible, illegal immigrants and child laborers are particularly vulnerable due to fear of deportation or other legal troubles.

GET YOUR V ON

Hmmm . . . bad for starving humans, bad for human rights, bad for our health, bad for the animals, bad for the planet. Why do we eat animal products? Because they taste good. I get it. And so many of us, myself included, are ruled by our taste buds. The good news is, and I've experienced this first-hand, our taste buds change. And so does our brain chemistry. Unhealthy foods can lose their appeal, and healthy foods can become more enticing. It really does happen. But like any addiction, we need some space and time away from the "drug" before we can start to see clearly. Dr. Neal Barnard, president of the Physicians Committee for Responsible Medicine (PCRM), has written a great book that talks about how the brain works when it comes to food—*Breaking the Food Seduction*. (He actually has a lot of great books that are all interesting, easy to read, and pretty life-altering.) It was really helpful to understand why I was so cracked out on cheese when I quit eating it. So if you're ready to put your meat- or dairy-crackpipe down, I suggest trying a monthlong "veg pledge" just to see what it's like. Pick one month, plan ahead, get prepared, and try eating vegetarian or vegan for just thirty days of your life. There's a great website—GoVeg.com—that will even send you a free vegetarian starter kit to help kick things off. Chances are you've been a meat-eater your whole life. Wouldn't it be interesting to see how you feel and what would change if you went veg for one month of your life? When I first made the leap, I missed meat. But once I got over that hump, I felt healthier, happier, more positive, and I had more energy. And my body felt stronger and leaner and cleaner. Now, it's been nineteen years since I went veg and nine since I went vegan, and I have zero interest in eating animal products.

I feel like I'd be remiss if I didn't address the *idea* of veganism here. For me, the V-word means compassion and a willingness to put principles above desires. But I know that for many people, veganism and vegetarianism mean something else—something weird and annoying and radical and fringe. Veganism never hired a good publicist, so some people think it's lame, creepy, or miserable. But if you search as far back into your mental files as you can, you'll likely see there's no real foundation for this mindset at all. Yes, there are some lame, creepy, miserable vegans, but there are plenty of lame, creepy, miserable meat-eaters too, right? My normal, cool vegan friends and I request that you don't judge an entire cause by its freaks. Every movement's got 'em. Most of us simply care about animals, care about our health, and care about our planet. We're just like you. The only difference is we've made the decision to align our actions with our beliefs. And we hope you'll join us and do the same.

BACK TO SCHOOL

So there I was, nineteen years old, unfortunate hair, in college, reading that article about factory farming and slaughterhouses, and looking at the pictures. I had never once thought about how animals went from living, feeling beings to meat. But PETA had gotten the information into my hands and the truth was inescapable. I sobbed for the animals and felt sick, enraged, and frantic. How could this go on? How could I have been a part of it all this time? And how could I stop it? I knew in that moment that I could never eat another cow, chicken, or pig ever again. Or wear one. I quickly set out trying to explain what happened to animals to everyone I knew; I felt desperate to stop the slaughter of animals. Some people listened; some people didn't. Some people, like my animal-loving parents—God bless them—swore off meat, too. About a year later, I got another PETA magazine in the mail. This time there was an article about fish and how they feel pain; I never ate fish again. I graduated college as a vegetarian, and some years later, stopped eating eggs and drinking milk, too.

Around my ten-year anniversary as a vegetarian, I was at an event for Farm Sanctuary when they showed undercover video footage taken at a dairy farm. There were all these cows, tripping, stumbling, and falling, either sick, lame, or both. Their udders were so grotesquely swollen, they were dragging on the ground. I knew in that moment, I could never eat cheese again and feel okay about it. I finally got past my cheese addiction and became totally vegan.

Fast-forward a few years. Remember my BFF from college, Tracy Silverman? Her sister, Lauren, had also become my BFF by then. The Silverman sisters bought us tickets to a forum that Farm Sanctuary was hosting in Trenton, New Jersey. At the time, Tracy had graduated from law school and was getting litigation experience so she could get a job as an animal rights attorney. Lauren had just completed an internship with the Humane Society of the United States and was in her second year of law school—she was going to become a lobbyist for animals. I was an agent at Ford Models in NYC. I was making six figures a year; I owned a home with Reggie; and my life seemed all mapped out. But I had been growing increasingly unfulfilled with my job. I was impressed with and inspired by the Silverman sisters—that their lives were set up that they could make the world a better place for animals. I had just started reading *The Artist's Way* by Julia Cameron, and this John Burroughs quote had really stuck out:

"Leap and the net will appear." I had read something else that said when we find our true calling and go after it, the universe conspires to help us. And I had just finished reading *Real Magic* by Dr. Wayne Dyer and was blown away. He wrote about *satori,* the state of sudden indescribable intuitive enlightenment.[406] As I sat next to the Silverman sisters in the Farm Sanctuary conference, it became crystal clear to me: "If I feel this strongly about animals and I'm not doing anything to help them, then who will?" I turned to Tracy and Lauren within minutes of the start of the conference and said, "I'm quitting my job to become an animal rights activist."

A WINDY ROAD

I got back to work on Monday and gave them my notice. I didn't care if I went from making $100,000 a year to making $17,000 a year—I knew I was fulfilling my destiny and that the universe would provide for me. My plan was to get a job at any animal rights organization. Except none were hiring. Thankfully, Reggie and I had saved a decent amount of money. So I became a pro bono animal rights activist—I went to demonstrations and protests; I volunteered at fundraisers; I called legislators; and I wrote letters to editors of newspapers and magazines. A year or so later, Reggie and I started to realize that we might not be soul mates after all. When we decided to part ways, we had gone through most of our savings, and I knew I needed to get a paying job again. I was devastated to give up on being an animal rights activist, but I felt like the universe wasn't holding up its end of the bargain; it was supposed to conspire to help me.

I decided that if I couldn't help animals, than I would try and manipulate children into helping animals. I would become a teacher. I set out on that path with a heavy heart but determined to make the best of it. I got a job working at a preschool and kindergarten enrichment program. Whenever I could, I told the kids that Ms. Freedman was a vegan, that Ms. Freedman didn't wear fur, and that Ms. Freedman would never buy a dog from a pet store. And when we were creating a Thanksgiving play, I suggested that Thomas the Turkey was the star, the farmer who wanted to kill Thomas the Turkey was the villain, and that the kids who kidnapped Thomas and saved him from slaughter were the heroes. I did the best I could, but the reality was, I wasn't into kids at all. I was meant to be an animal rights activist.

Little did I know, the universe *had been* conspiring to help me all that time. Every morning, while driving to work, I was listening to Tony Robbins' *Hour of Power* and *Get the Edge* CDs that my friend Julie had lent me. He talked about the power of goal setting, and it had a huge impact on me. At some point during that time period, I'd had the idea to write a "diet" book about veganism. I followed Tony's directions for goal setting, and on my list of goals that I had to accomplish in one year or less was "write *Skinny Bitch*." (One of the other goals was to get my Spanish up and running, and I can't remember the third. I did buy a Spanish book, but my real mojo got spent on *Skinny Bitch*.) I thought that if regular people learned about factory farming and slaughterhouses, maybe they'd be as horrified as I was and stop eating animals. But I also knew that no one wanted to read this type of doom and gloom, and that no one willingly gave up their favorite foods. I also knew that women were obsessed with being thin. It was at this intersection that *Skinny Bitch* was born. I didn't sit down with a pen and paper and try to come up with a catchy title—it just appeared in my brain. From the universe.

Days after deciding that I was going to write a book, I had dinner with friends whom I hadn't seen in years. When they asked what I was up to and I told them, they announced they were writing a book and that I should contact their literary agent. The universe was on a roll now. Within a few months of deciding to write a book, I landed an agent and publishing deal. (I had also decided to quit my teaching job and move from New Jersey to Los Angeles.)

Skinny Bitch came out in December of 2005 to little fanfare. I thought that for sure, with such a provocative title, it would get tons of press. It got almost none. Through word of mouth, though, the book was selling well and had become an *LA Times* best seller. But it wasn't until a fateful day about a year and a half after its initial release that *Skinny Bitch* hit it big. While in Los Angeles filming a reality TV special, Victoria Beckham was photographed holding the book. A huge media frenzy ensued—*Skinny Bitch* went from getting zero publicity to getting tons, overnight. (I'll never forget: I was on the rowing machine at the gym when my editor called to tell me that *Skinny Bitch* was on the *New York Times* Best Seller list. I cried.) I don't know her stance on animal rights issues, but I'm thankful for Victoria Beckham's inadvertent participation in helping advance the vegan message.

If you're interested in getting more in-depth info about vegan eating, check out *Skinny Bitch* (for women), *Skinny Bastard (*for men), or *Skinny Bitch: Bun in the Oven* (for preggers). I never set out to be a writer, but alas, I think they're pretty good books. I set out to be an animal rights activist, and the universe conspired to help me.

YOUR TURN

So now you know my story. What's yours? Are you willing to take on the challenge of trying something new? Something potentially life-altering in ways you can't begin to dream of? Are you willing to live a life that matches your principles, even if it feels like a sacrifice at first? Even if it means being uncomfortable at the beginning?

For me, motivation and inspiration are everything. So I highly recommend getting as educated and inspired as possible. I offer a list of books and videos in Chapter Eleven. But probably the best motivation of all is actually meeting some animals. There are rescue sanctuaries all over the world. (I list a few of my faves in Chapter Eleven, too.) Find one near you and meet these animals face to face. See who it is you'd be eating.

CALL IN REINFORCEMENTS

Sometimes the despair of what's happening to animals all over the world makes me want to dig a hole, crawl in, and die. But thankfully, I'm surrounded by amazing and beautiful vegan friends, who care enough to try and make the world a better place for animals. The sage yogi Yogananda once said, "Environment is stronger than willpower."[407] Having a vegan community is really important, so do what you can to get friends and family on the bus with you. Lend them this book; invite them to do the thirty-day "veg pledge" with you; plan vegan potlucks—whatever it takes to make sure you're not alone in this endeavor. It really does make things a lot easier if you have a support system in place. I've never looked into them myself, but I'm told there are a ton of veggie meetup groups. Join one (www.meetup.com), volunteer at or attend animal rights events in your 'hood, get involved. That said, even if you're the only vegan in a 100-mile radius, you can still do it. For many years, Tracy was my only veg friend, and we didn't always live in the same state. Where there's a will, there's a way. And where there's good vegan food, there are vegans. Happycow.net will tell you where the veg-friendly restaurants and stores are in your neck of the woods. I've used it all over the world; it's my go-to every time I travel.

Don't let anyone bring you down. There will likely be haters or people who have a negative reaction to your new way of being. Understandably, it's confronting for people when those around them adopt an elevated way of life that they're not ready for yet. It sometimes threatens people or makes them feel bad about themselves. This sometimes results in them making stupid, boring meat jokes or policing your lifestyle. "How about a nice, juicy steak?" "Your shoes are leather." "You can't eat that, it has butter in it!" Don't engage in any negativity. If they're open to having an intelligent conversation, great. You can share what you've learned, what you've decided, and what you're doing about it. But it isn't a debate. You don't need to convince them of anything or sell them on anything. You don't need their approval, and you don't need to convert them. It's simply your job to be a beacon of light of compassion, dignity, health, and grace. Stay on your path, and allow them to be on theirs.

And feel excited about this path! Veganism is exciting, and so is making big life changes. Veganism is a portal for everything good to come in your life and in the world. Enjoy food, enjoy being healthy, and enjoy feeling great. But most of all, enjoy sparing animals from pain, suffering, confinement, and cruelty. If you want to send me hate mail about duping you into reading about veganism, feel free. But I'd much prefer to hear that got your free vegetarian starter kit from GoVeg.com, and that you're trying a thirty-day veg pledge.

Are you really an animal lover, or just a pet lover? Ch-ch-ch-changes . . .

"Three things in human life are important: the first is to be kind; the second is to be kind; and the third is to be kind."

—HENRY JAMES

CHAPTER 11

LET'S GET PHYSICAL

*O*kay, time to get down to the brass tacks of making these ch-ch-ch-changes. Having been a dog parent for over twelve years, I've got some wisdom to share. Don't get me wrong: I'm far from being a Stepford mom. I'm impatient and selfish all the time. And when I'm nearing a project deadline, I totally neglect my dogs' needs. And even though I live in Los Angeles, I almost never take them to the beach. That said, I am a pretty good mom. So here are some dos and don'ts for other dog parents.

Oh, and having been a cat mom for four years, a vegetarian and animal rights activist since 1994, and vegan since 2004, I've also got some other animal-related wisdom to share. Allow me to be your animal guru.

DO

....

Do adopt animals instead of purchasing them. (If you didn't get that from the first few chapters, I give up.) This doesn't just mean dogs and cats, but small animals too, like gerbils, hamsters, guinea pigs, rabbits, etc. These animals can also suffer in breeding operations and pet stores.

Do spay and neuter. (Again, this is a given at this point.)

Do help others spay and neuter their pets. In low-income communities, some people will acquire animals, not spay or neuter them, and then either bring them to the shelter, give them away, or ditch them in a parking lot. (To be fair, some people in high-income communities also do this.) If you want to help and have the funds to do so, you can "sponsor" spay and neuter programs. Google it. Many people who couldn't otherwise afford to spay or neuter their animals take advantage of these opportunities when they're offered.

Do be aware that many animals get so freaked out by fireworks that the day after firework holidays, shelters have a huge influx. Animals get so scared, they break out of their homes and run away. So do what you have to do to make sure your animals are safe and comforted, even if it means staying home with them.

Do carefully trim any hair that's blocking their eyes. How would you like it if you couldn't see, due to overgrown bangs? Just be sure to check with a groomer or vet first, because sometimes trimming the hair will make it poke the dogs in the eyes. Sometimes, believe it or not, tying the hair back might be a better solution, depending on the breed.

Do brush your animals regularly. The more hair you can get off their bodies and into the brush, the less hair they'll barf up later. It's also good for their circulation and helps keep their skin from getting smelly, dirty buildup. And, it's a nice bonding time for you and the fur-spring.

Do talk to your animals all the time. I don't mean mindless drivel about your job; I mean explaining where you're going and when you'll be back. Or if you're traveling, letting them know and telling them who's going to stay with them. Or if they're going to the vet, that they're safe and loved and that it's all okay. They have an amazing capacity to understand tone, body language, and cadence. They may not initially understand the words, but they often have at least a sense of what you're saying.

Do consider their feelings and needs before making plans. If dogs only get a rushed walk before work, then you're away all day, then they get a rushed walk when you get home, and then you go out again for the night—that's not great parenting. Ignoring them for the few hours you're home or rushing to go out again isn't kind or considerate. They need to play, have quality time with you, quality time outside. On days when you're really busy, hire a dog walker, send them to doggie daycare, or ask for help from a friend or neighbor.

Do be available for emotional intimacy with your dogs. Yes, it's nice to mindlessly pet them while watching TV or talking on the phone, but it's important to also have quiet moments when you're just petting them, *really* being with them, and focusing all your love and attention on them. I make a point of spending a few minutes with each of my dogs every morning before getting out of bed and every night before going to sleep. One at a time, they each get to feel that loving soul connection. (Of course, they also get multiple love-maulings throughout the day, too.)

Do share dogs with exes. It works great for all parties involved. It will make your life easier, and the dog's life happier. And don't be afraid to think outside the box and share a dog with a neighbor or your siblings.

Do offer to walk, hike, or babysit other people's dogs if you don't have your own. Especially if the dog's parent is disabled, elderly, single, or overwhelmed with children. While you're at it, do it for your neglectful and lazy neighbors, too. It doesn't matter whether they have good or bad reasons for not taking their dogs out, just help the dogs.

Do let people you trust know that your dogs can be "borrowed." When I first moved to LA and was still getting used to being a single mom, I had three angelic neighbors who would take my dogs for walks and hikes. It was a godsend, knowing my dogs were out having fun and being loved on, and I could relax at home, run a few errands, or go out with a clear conscience. (Thank you and bless you Chris, Gianina, and Katarina.)

Do test their dog beds to make sure they're comfortable. Sometimes they are thin on the bottom, and it's almost like they're sleeping on the hard floor itself. Not a very nice thing to do to our best friends.

Do brush their teeth and have their teeth cleaned professionally. There are doggie dental hygienists who will come to your home and clean their teeth without anesthesia.

Do clean their ears.

Do check the tightness of their collars regularly. Imagine if you had to spend every day of your life in a necktie or necklace that was too tight? Conversely, loose collars can slip off in the middle of intersections.

Do let them be naked at home sometimes. (I'm hesitant to include this because, God forbid, something could happen—like a fire, an earthquake, or even something less dramatic, like forgetting to put the collar back on—and your beloved can get outside without a name tag. But if you feel like you can handle the responsibility and the world is safe, it might be nice to let them lounge around nude on occasion.)

Do ask to stay in the room with your dog at the vet. Letting them get carted off to the back room to have blood drawn or other procedures is unfair. (I'm not talking about emergency situations or surgeries.) They're already scared just being at the vet—don't wimp out on them and send them off to get worked on. Unless you are hysterical and stressing your pet out, reasonable and professional vets should have no problem with this request. Don't be scared to advocate for your beloved child.

Do feed them good-quality food and food that they like. Imagine if you ate the same food every single day of your life, and you hated it. Don't just give them kibble and canned food every day. They need and deserve some fresh food, too. Carrots, bananas, and apples (no apple seeds, though) make great snacks. And provided you don't have one of those dogs with a crazy-sensitive stomach, beans, yams, spinach, red cabbage, and broccoli are all good additions.* Check with your vet before altering their diets.

*In order to avoid an influx of emails asking what I feed my dogs, here goes:

A blend of V-Dog kibble (they ship for free), beans, whole grains, and Preference (made by the Honest Kitchen). Preference is green slop—a blend of alfalfa, potatoes, fruits, and veggies, rehydrated with water. I also like to change things up and add in a spoonful of ground flax seeds or nutritional yeast or a drizzle of oil. And depending on what fresh veggies I have in the fridge, they might get some of that added in. (Some human foods are dangerous for dogs, so don't go dumping your fridge contents into their bowls without doing your research first.)

Do let them eat pesticide-free wild grass; it's part of their natural diet.

Do hire a trainer if there's some behavioral stuff going on. Most problems can be easily fixed with the help of a professional. And usually, *we* are the problem, not the dogs. A few bucks now can save you a lifetime of annoying, frustrating behavior.

Do check out this great website before treating your animals for fleas and ticks: www.simplesteps.org/greenpaws-products (Thank you, Julie Morris.)

Do understand that your dog might eat poo, roll in it, or rub it on the face/neck/ear region. It happens sometimes.

Do expect your dog to pee, poop, and puke all over your house, and try to have a sense of humor about it. It may not happen, but if it does, you'll have known it was always a possibility, and you won't be a mean, yelling jerk.

Do foster a pet. Even if you don't keep him or her, it's such a rewarding experience to help animals in need.

Do give money to rescue groups or individuals. They are unsung heroes.

Do what you can to help. If you can't adopt an animal, foster. If you can't foster, sponsor, by paying for food and vet bills for the foster family or rescue group. If you can't sponsor, help find homes for those in need.

Do volunteer at shelters.

Do consider adopting the "undesirable" dogs and cats at shelters. Most people want puppies and kittens, so they're the most adoptable. Animals who are old, disabled, blind, deaf, missing a limb, or require medication are often disregarded. They need love as much as, if not more than, the young ones. (Plus, a well-known fact among animal advocates: seniors are so much easier than puppies. They are long past their wild, destructive, peeing-and-pooping-everywhere phase.)

Do be mindful as to what kind of animal you have. If she's a social butterfly and wants to come everywhere with you (and can handle herself), bring her along whenever you can. If he's fearful or grumpy and would rather be left alone, don't drag him to your family picnic. Also be mindful of the temperature and environment. Dragging your dog to the town parade in ninety-degree heat isn't fun for even the most social of dogs.

Do be conscious of whether your animal wants to be an only child or have siblings. If you see two cats who are already bonded, why not adopt them both? And if your dog seems bored or lonely and loves other dogs, rescue a sister for him. Conversely, if your fur-spring really hates other animals, don't subject her to your whims. (Timber and Joey fall into the "dislike other animals" category, but not "hate." And because Lucy is small and submissive, she's somewhat irrelevant to them. But if your animal is really scared or really unhappy about other animals, honor his or her feelings.)

Do remember to honor all these precious beings. They are such gifts to us in every way. Will we ever have a more loyal, faithful, accepting, loving, forgiving friend? Remember to cherish them, show them you're grateful, and give them the food, time, love, and attention they want and deserve.

Do tell them it's okay to "go" when they are nearing death. They're so loyal and faithful they may be hanging on just to please you. But if they're suffering or at the end of their lives, it's more humane to give them your blessing to cross over.

DON'T

....

Don't let your children torment your dog just because your dog tolerates it.

Don't store your dog's food in the same cabinet as your laundry detergent or other cleansers. How would you like if it your dinner smelled and tasted like chemical fragrance? (Now multiply that times a thousand, because that's how much stronger their senses of smell are than ours.)

Don't forget that dogs have free will. Training them doesn't mean that we have the right to get what we want from them. It means we patiently share with them what makes us happy and then praise them generously for doing it. We should be grateful for every small thing they do to please us.

Don't hit your dog. Ever. It's not a method of training or teaching; it's you expressing frustration. Any book or trainer that says you should roll up a newspaper and hit your dog on the nose is off the mark. Corporal punishment is not acceptable.

Don't scream at animals. Showing a little disappointment goes a long way and more than adequately conveys the message. Screaming doesn't help them or you; it's just you being unable to control your anger.

Don't kick them out of your room at bedtime. Other than a few independent ones, most dogs want to be with us all the time, even when we sleep. Hours spent in the same room, even while sleeping, count as hours logged together. It matters to them.

Don't have furniture they're not allowed on. Their lives are so small as it is; they spend more time home than you do. Imagine if you weren't allowed on the most comfortable couch in the house. Really, imagine it. It's awful. (You can keep a blanket or sheet on the couch and take it off when you have company.)

Don't rush them on their walks. It's the few times a day that they get to experience being alive. Yes, we're all busy and sometimes we don't allot enough time to go from one thing to another. But our dogs are forced to live according to our schedules in every way. Surely we can let them really own the measly three walks they get daily.

Don't bring your phone on your walks. Try and actually be present with your dog; don't phone it in. Even though I'm guilty of it too sometimes, it's sad when people are walking their dogs absentmindedly, so distracted by their conversation they're tugging them along without thinking. Enjoy the outdoors with your dog. It'll make you both happier, more connected, and will remind you that your dog is a feeling being, and not a set prop in your life. It may also be the few times per day your aren't tethered to your phone—try to enjoy it!

Don't be on the phone when you first get home. Really be present with them. They've been waiting all day to see you, and they deserve some intimate connection and attention before you get busy with making dinner, etc.

Don't use choke chains or pinch collars. Yes, sometimes (or all the time) dogs pull. It's annoying, maddening, and even hazardous on occasion. But there are other options—like Haltis and Gentle Leaders—that aren't as cruel, oppressive, and potentially dangerous. At a dog park I used to frequent, I was told about two dogs who were playing and wrestling when one's tooth got caught in the choke collar of the other. Despite frantic attempts by the panicked dogs and their horrified humans to detach them, the dog wearing the choke collar died. Harnesses are much better options. And so is dog training. Timber and Joey used to drag me around like a rag doll, until a little simple training I picked up watching TV made a world of difference.

Don't be a "no" parent. It's so sad when I'm hiking or at the dog park and some controlling parent is stopping their dog from doing everything. They aren't toddlers—they're dogs. They're going to bark, run, sniff, jump, hump, chase, eat grass, dig holes, chew sticks, and get dirty. Let them. Yes, if you know your dog barfs every time he eats grass, wanting to redirect him is understandable. But screaming "NO!" every ten seconds isn't the best way to do it. Having a killjoy for a parent sucks for the dog.

Don't overfeed your dog; it's misplaced love. I know, I know, many of them always seem hungry. I have Labs—let's leave it at that. But it's our job as parents to feed them an appropriate amount of food and not fall prey to their puppy-dog eyes. They're master manipulators. Don't kill them with kindness: carrying around extra weight is as unhealthy for dogs as it is for humans.

Don't ever let them walk on escalators. I know two separate people who brought their Chihuahuas on escalators, and their toes got caught and seriously injured. When they brought their dogs to their respective vets, both vets said it's a common problem.

Don't get them dyed for Halloween or for any other ludicrous reason. Most dogs do not like going to the groomer as it is. Subjecting them to additional time there and having their hair tugged at, just so you can get attention via your dog, isn't very kind. If you actually stayed and watched the whole process and saw how miserable your dog was, you'd feel terrible. And don't do it yourself at home, either. Exposing their skin to chemicals is a bad idea (skin is the body's largest organ), even before taking into account that they lick themselves.

Don't wash your dog with anything with fragrance. Their sense of smell is astronomically strong. How would you feel if you were doused in some cheap, gross perfume and couldn't get rid of the smell for days?

Don't be a breedist (the animal equivalent to racist). There are millions of pit bulls, Rottweilers, and Dobermans who are as sweet as golden retrievers. Discriminating against them or the people who parent them is wrong.

Don't be a crate-head. Cramming your dog into a cage for ten straight hours is wrong, wrong, wrong. Hire a dog walker, work something out with a friend or neighbor, or share custody with your ex. Dogs deserve better than home-jail.

Don't keep your dog tied up. It's literally maddening to them, and can incite frustration, anger, and even attacks. All justifiably so. Build a fenced-in yard, take them to off-leash parks, or figure something else out.

Don't make them hold their bowels and bladders for absurdly long periods of time. Just because they can doesn't mean they should. Try to figure your schedule out better.

Don't scream at them to "shut up" when they're barking at someone outside. Calmly explain who it is and why they don't need to bark. (I'm still working on this one.)

Don't ever leave your dog's leash on him when leaving him in the car or anywhere else unattended. He can easily get it caught on something and choke or hang himself.

Don't fly your animals in the cargo holds of airplanes. It's stressful, scary, and dangerous. Most cargo holds don't have regulated temperature or adequate ventilation, and they're exposed to loud engine noise. The USDA, which is responsible for animal safety on airplanes admits, "virtually every major airline has been cited and fined for repeatedly mishandling animals."[408] And virtually every major airline has had animal injuries or deaths.[409] Figure out an alternative.

Don't put your cat's litter box next to her food and water dishes. How would you like eating your meals next to a dirty toilet?

Don't buy leashes or collars made of leather. Killing cows for dog collars is like robbing Peter to pay Paul, only meaner, because killing is worse than stealing.

Don't have birds as pets (unless he or she is a rescue who can't be released into the wild). Is there anything more horrible than taking animals who are meant to *fly*, clipping their wings, and keeping them caged?

Don't set lethal traps for mice and rats. And don't use glue traps, either, which can rip off their fur and skin, cause them to break or chew their legs off, or cause them to die from starvation, dehydration, or suffocation. There are humane traps that will allow you to catch and release these innocent creatures.

Don't kill bugs—relocate them. Mercy is mercy, whether it's for a dog or a spider. Why would you ever choose death when mercy is an option?

NUTS AND BOLTS

Like the fish who can't see the water they're living in because it's all around them, our exploitation of animals is just as pervasive. We buy and sell them like toys, wear their skins, eat their flesh, and walk past their misery, suffering, and death every day without a second's thought. This book is an invitation to have a radical awakening regarding animals. To be the fish that sees the water. And to be a *real* animal lover (not just a dog and cat lover).

So what's it gonna be? You're either in or you're out.

I'm gonna assume you're in. Hopefully you're invigorated and motivated and ready to jump in with both feet. I know it may seem daunting to completely change your life, but don't let it overwhelm you. You can do this. Some stuff will be easy, some stuff might be hard. Whatever. You'll figure it out. In the meantime, here's some *animal activism* 101:

If you or someone you know loses an animal, call your local animal services department, police department, state troopers, highway patrol, and local rescue groups. Go to all your shelters daily; do not call. It's much better to show up in person and see for yourself. People who find dogs sometimes bring them to vets, animal hospitals, groomers, kennels, and even pet stores. Visit them all. If your animal has a tag with your contact information, chances are good that someone will get in touch with you. That said, don't sit around waiting. Be proactive and be fast about it. Hang posters nearby, hand out fliers, and check and put listings on craigslist.org under "lost and found." Use social media sites like Facebook to post pictures and info about the missing animal. Ask friends to spread the word and ask for help searching. Google "when you've lost your pet" for some helpful articles on the subject. Petharbor.com is a great resource if you lose or find an animal (or if you're looking to adopt).

Pawproject.org is a great resource and nonprofit organization leading the fight to ban declawing.

Dog racing needs to be abolished. You can be part of the solution by never going to dog races, educating your friends and family, and visiting the website of Grey2KUSA.org, which is leading the fight against greyhound racing.

GoVeg.com, TryVeg.com, and ChooseVeg.com all offer free vegetarian starter kits. Get one ASAP!

Here are some of my favorite nonprofit organizations that help animals. Most of them have action alerts on their websites where you can sign petitions, send emails, or make phone calls on behalf of animals. It's a fast, easy, and effective way to influence change:

- Animal Aid Unlimited

- Animal Legal Defense Fund

- Beagle Freedom Project

- Chimp Rescue

- The CIA Club (Compassion in Action, for students)

- Compassion Over Killing

- Farm Sanctuary

- The Humane Society of the United States

- In Defense of Animals

- Mercy for Animals

- PETA

- PETA2 (for kids and young adults)

- Physicians Committee for Responsible Medicine (PCRM)

- Sea Shepherd

- Stray Cat Alliance

- Woodstock Farm Animal Sanctuary

I highly recommend getting on their email lists. They'll send you timely action alerts so you can help animals in seconds flat with a few mouse clicks. (If this book changes your life and you want to thank me, feel free to make a donation to any of these nonprofits. It's all the thanks I want or need.)

Use Facebook to help animals. You can post all sorts of stuff educating your friends and family about the ways you're being a better animal lover. And you can share petitions and action alerts.

Guess what? You just became an animal rights activist! Isn't it easy and so rewarding? Signing up with the animal groups, signing their petitions, and then posting their stuff on Facebook or other social media sites are among the most effective things you can do as an armchair activist. Really.

Don't stop now. You can email these embassies and tell them you oppose the barbaric bloodsport of bullfighting and that it has a negative impact on their country's image and tourism:

Embassy of Spain
emb.washington@maec.es

Embassy of Mexico
mexembusa@sre.gob.mx

Embassy of France
info@ambafrance-us.org

Embassy of Portugal
mail@scwas.dgaccp.pt

And if you ever see a company or travel magazine advertising or glorifying bullfighting, be sure to send them a quick email telling them you're opposed to the murdering of innocent animals. It will take you all of one minute, but it could mean major change for bulls.

If you want to be more than an armchair activist, another bonus of getting on the mailing lists of various animal rights groups is that they'll let you know when there are protests, events, and demonstrations in your neighborhood. So, for example, if a store that sells puppy mill dogs is in your town, you can show up with other like-minded animal lovers, hand out leaflets educating customers, and effect change. It's also a great way to meet like-minded people and be part of your local animal rights community.

Shannon Mann's boundless passion and tireless dedication is an inspiration to me and to people all over the world. While most of us may not be willing to risk our lives for months at a time on a ship in the Antarctic, or spend our precious "down time" doing nonstop rescue work and investigations, we can still do our parts. Shannon recently launched an amazing site to help us do just that: backyardactivist.com. It localizes activists geographically, so you can get involved with issues in your own backyard. *Genius*.

Whenever I see people wearing fur, I tell them (as nicely as I can) that I used to think fur was pretty until I learned what happened to the animals. And then I suggest that they educate themselves, so if they decide to continue wearing fur, they'll at least know what it is they're contributing to. (Admittedly, it doesn't always go well.) I was honored to participate in the award-winning documentary, *Skin Trade*, and I highly recommend it to anyone looking for a more in-depth look at the fur industry.

If your city still allows horse carriages, contact your city officials and tell them you're vehemently opposed. Check out the documentary *Blinders* if you need help convincing them. The film's website, blindersthemovie.com, has a "what you can do" link.

When animal circuses come to your town, go! Just don't buy a ticket. Stand outside with other protesters and educate patrons with leaflets and signs. (Both will be provided by animal rights organizations leading the demo, but feel free to make your own.) Ask your local council members to enact a ban on animal circuses in your town. It's happening all over the world. And support nonanimal circuses that feature talented and willing human performers.

It's not enough for us to avoid rodeos. We need to let the sponsors of these events know we are horrified by their contributions and that we'll be boycotting their brands while they continue supporting cruelty.

When buying products of any kind, check the labels to make sure they're cruelty-free. No animal ingredients and no animal testing. Yay! See how easy it is to be a conscious consumer? If a label doesn't say or you don't know what an ingredient is, call the company's number then and there, ask them about the ingredient or animal testing, and be sure to tell them your purchasing policy. Together, we do make a difference. (If you want to do some preemptive reconnaissance, Google "compassionate consumer guide.")

When buying shoes, purses, bags, belts, jackets, and wallets, simply read the label. If it says leather, barf, and put the item back. If it says "synthetic" or "man-made materials," you've just discovered vegan fashion. See how easy it was? Just like in the regular shoe and purse world, vegan shoes and purses come at every price point. We've got Stella McCartney and Mink for those who like fancy shmancies, middle-of-the-road prices but awesome looks by Matt & Nat, Olsenhaus, Beyond Skin, and Cri de Coeur, and tons of cheapies that are "accidentally vegan." Even huge online retailers like Zappos and Amazon, and brick-and-mortar stores like Payless and Target, have a vegan selection.

Compassion is the fashion. Check out vautecouture.com for some hipster-chic women's wear. Bravegentleman.com has men covered for everything cruelty-free and cool; it's one-stop shopping. Herbivoreclothing.com has some cool message shirts that you can sport with pride. And

AlternativeOutfitters.com has a little bit of everything.

Girliegirlarmy.com, thediscerningbrute.com, kathyfreston.com, kriscarr.com, and mainstreetvegan.net are fun, interesting sites to visit and have mailing lists that you can get on. Compassionatecook.com and ourhenhouse.org are popular, well-liked podcasts.

The best way to put a stop to the Iditarod dog sledding race once and for all is to contact the sponsors of the race and tell them you'll be boycotting their products or services until they withdraw their support permanently. For a current list of who's contributing to this horrid race, Google "Iditarod sponsors."

For anything and everything related to dog training, I recommend tamargeller.com.

Maybe some of you (Jews) are thinking Kosher equals humane? Undercover video footage taken from the largest kosher slaughterhouse in the world says otherwise. Investigations in 2004 and 2008 both revealed violent and hideous violations.[410] (You can visit HumaneKosher.com for more info.)

Go meet some animals. Here are some of my favorite sanctuaries. If you don't live near these, find one near you:

- Animal Acres in Acton, California (just outside Los Angeles)

- Catskill Animal Sanctuary in Saugerties, New York

- Farm Sanctuary in Orland, California and Watkins Glen, New York

- Poplar Spring Animal Sanctuary in Poolesville, Maryland

- Woodstock Farm Animal Sanctuary in Woodstock, New York

If you need extra motivation with this new way of life, check out the PETA videos narrated by Pink (wool), Alec Baldwin (circuses), Joaquin Phoenix (exotic skins), James Cromwell (meat), Paul McCartney (meat), and Pamela Anderson (leather). Another must-watch is the video, "Whose Skin are You In?". And the ninety-minute film *Earthlings*, narrated by Joaquin Phoenix, will leave you forever changed. It is incredibly powerful and it covers many of the issues discussed in this book.

If you're ready to get educated about vegetarianism and veganism, check out the films *Vegucated* and *Forks Over Knives*. Both are awesome. I highly recommend any and all books written by John Robbins and Drs. Neal Barnard, Caldwell Esselstyn, T. Colin Campbell, John McDougall, Dean Ornish, Michael Greger, and Joel Fuhrman. PCRM.org is also a great resource. These are names you can trust in the world of health and diet. Some more recommended reading:

If you're _____, read _____:

- athletic: Brendan Brazier's *Thrive*

- intellectual: Jonathan Safran Foer's *Eating Animals*

- a feminist: Carol J. Adams's *The Sexual Politics of Meat*

- a yogi/yogini: Sharon Gannon's *Yoga and Vegetarianism*

- spiritual: Will Tuttle's *The World Peace Diet*

- Christian: Matthew Scully's *Dominion*

- open to cursing, laughing, and learning at the same time: *Skinny Bitch* or *Skinny Bastard*

- easing in to the lifestyle: Kathy Freston's *The Lean*

- just plain cool: Kris Carr's *Crazy Sexy Diet*

- looking to get your veg on with a lovely lady: Victoria Moran's *The Love-Powered Diet* or *Main Street Vegan*

- someone who likes to laugh, cry, and be inspired: Jenny Brown and Gretchen Primack's *The Lucky Ones*

- a lover of animal stories: Kathy Stevens's *Animal Camp* or *Where the Blind Horse Sings*

- appreciative of a really smart, comprehensive read: Karen Dawn's *Thanking the Monkey*

- open to reading about the correlation of our treatment of animals with the Holocaust: Charles Patterson's *Eternal Treblinka*

- into recipes, interesting articles, and staying in the know: *VegNews* magazine

And if you want to read the classics—the ones that started it all: *The Jungle* (1906) by Upton Sinclair, *Animal Liberation* (1975, second edition 2009) by Peter Singer, *Animal Theology* (1994) by Andrew Linzey, *The Food Revolution* (2001) by John Robbins, and *Fast Food Nation* (2005) by Eric Schlosser. Also very compelling, interesting, and important: Peter Singer and Jim Mason's *The Way We Eat*; *The Inner World of Farm Animals* by Amy Hatkoff, and all of Jeffrey Moussaieff Masson's many books on animals. And a beautiful, moving book of photography and rescued animal stories—*Ninety-Five: Meeting America's Animals in Stories and Photographs* (edited by No Voice Unheard).

If you're already committed to the veg lifestyle and want to support outreach efforts to get others on the bus, visit VeganOutreach.org. And read *The Animal Activist's Handbook* by Matt Ball and Bruce Friedrich.

So how exactly do you go vegan? First, order your veg starter kit, watch those movies, and read those books. Then, know you've got options for tackling your vegan conversion. If you're ready to dive in, go for it. If you need to go slowly, "lean in," like Kathy Freston says. A great way to do that is to take the thirty-day veg pledge. And beyond that, use simple common sense, one meal at a time. If you eat cereal for breakfast, just use soy milk, rice milk, almond milk, oat milk, or hempseed milk instead of cows' milk. If you normally eat a meat and cheese sandwich for lunch, swap the meat and cheese out for vegan versions. Yes, they exist. (In *Skinny Bitch* and *Skinny Bastard*, there are food lists and menu plans.) Everything you eat now exists in the vegan world, too. It's amazing. Go to your local health-food store and try new things. Or just start opening your eyes to the vegan foods that are available in the store you shop in now. Just take it one meal at a time. Don't freak yourself out. Have fun with it: Sporkonline.com offers online cooking classes if you want to create exciting vegan fare. Check out one of the thousands of vegan cookbooks or free vegan recipes online. And know that you can be the eater you are today in the vegan world. Meaning: if you're a junk food meat-eater, you can be a junk-food vegan. If you're a health nut meat-eater, you can be a health nut vegan. You can still be your meat-loving self; just be the vegan version!

These are just some basic, general resources and tips to get you started. Basic and general. Hopefully you're also a self-starter, because I don't have the time or patience for hand-holding. You're gonna have to take the ball from here and run with it. I went vegetarian in 1994, at the age of nineteen, in my pot-smoking prime. I did it without help, without the Internet, and without brain cells. If I could do it then, you can easily do it now. We're well into the twenty-first century—we've got options galore and the World Wide Web. If something isn't clear or you need more information, Google it, and leave me in peace. I've got three kids and I'm an animal rights activist; I don't have the interest or inclination to help you find a store near you that sells vegan corn dogs. Don't be a victim, be resourceful. If you can't find a store that sells vegan corn dogs, find one who will order them for you. If no one will, find a recipe online and make your own. If you don't cook and you want to live in a place that has vegan corn dogs, move.

I'm kidding, I'm kidding. *(Kind of.)* Yeah, being vegan is easier in certain areas. It's one of the reasons I moved from New Jersey to Los Angeles. But it certainly doesn't mean you have to move. Again, it's the twenty-first century. Maybe with the exception of Antarctica and some other extreme places, you can be vegan anywhere. My parents are vegans, and they still live in New Jersey and are obsessed with food. They eat like vegan royalty. I travel a lot, both domestically and internationally. And I eat all vegan food, with enthusiasm and gusto, everywhere I go. As I mentioned earlier, Happycow.net is my go-to; it tells you where all the veg-friendly food is, all over the world. (They've got an iPhone app. Another good one is Veg Out.)

Know that you may stumble along the way and not be a perfect vegan right out of the gate. Just remember who you are and who you want to be. And remember again, and again, and again. Keep coming back to your true north: your heart. Your heart wants only the best for you and for the world. Your heart will never say that you should eat a chicken sandwich, buy a pair of shoes, or go see a monkey movie. Your ego will have you desiring those things, needing them, and justifying them. Trust your heart. Listen carefully to the calling. The calling to be the vegan, animal rights activist you. The real you, the divine you.

Answer the call.

On behalf of the animals, I *Beg* you.

CHAPTER 12

LET'S GET SPIRITUAL

My editor thinks this chapter may be too "New Agey," too "woo woo," or "too religious" for readers. My literary agent thinks this chapter is possible fodder for negative book reviewers. I'm going rogue and keeping it anyway. You'll either get it and be into it, or you won't. Whatever. No big deal. Take what you like and leave the rest.

I'm going to talk about "God" now. Is that okay? I put quotation marks around God because it's such a loaded word; I don't want the God I'm talking about to be lumped in with the "God" that conjures up all sorts of negative reactions in people. I know I need to tread softly because there is so much baggage around "God." And I certainly see why—wars have been fought in "God's" name; hate and bigotry have been justified under "God"; and lots of people do lots of crazy things and attribute them to "God." Also, many people don't believe in "God," and they think that people who do are weird and/or stupid. So it's understandable and with good reason that people get a little squirrelly with the mention of "God." I do, too, sometimes. I don't want anyone pushing their "God" on me.

Today, at the age of thirty-eight, I have a relationship with the God of my understanding. And in my relationship and understanding, I refer to "God" by many names: God, the Divine, the Divine Mother, the Divine Father, Father/Mother God, and other names that I won't mention because they might raise eyebrows and distract from the point I'm making. The point is, whether you believe in a Judeo-Christian god, Buddhist Nirvana, Hindu gods, Allah, another god, or no god and no interest in getting one, there is something within in each of us that beckons us to a higher calling. It's a small seed planted in our hearts that won't die, despite how little nourishment it may get. I'm calling it God. But you can call it whatever you want and believe it to be whatever you want. As long as you know it's in there—that higher calling, that seed in your heart.

Why are we here? Why are we alive? Why are we in these bodies in this space and this time? I used to think the answer was "to be happy." And as I got older, "to be a good person," or "make the world a better place." But I've come to believe that we are here to attain enlightenment. To know our own true nature, the true nature of the world, and the purpose and meaning of life.[411] It's our purpose as individuals, and it's our purpose as a human race.

We all understand evolution from a physical perspective—we know that humans used to be grunting, hair-covered, barely upright cavemen. But it's not enough to evolve physically. We need to evolve emotionally, psychically, energetically, and spiritually, too. Not just for our own happiness or well-being, but for the greater good. And because it's who we were born to be. We did not come to these bodies and human experiences so we could mindlessly stuff food in our faces, watch TV, post stuff on Facebook, have sex, acquire property, collect possessions, wear cool clothes, and work out in gyms. We didn't even come here to birth and raise children, as high a calling as that might seem. We came here to remember our own divine nature. And then to remember it again. And again. And again.

Because it's easy to forget. It's why monks meditate in caves or retreat to monasteries, and why nuns sequester themselves in convents. They need to be away from earthly stuff to remember their true divine nature. Or they choose to be away from earthly stuff because they fall so deeply in love with the divine that they desire nothing else. This way of life may sound extreme, but this divinity is in all of us. That little seed planted in each of our hearts that refuses to die, despite how little of God's love we water it with—it's in all of us. Whether we have the strength or desire or fortitude to live divine, enlightened lives is a choice we must make every day—a choice we get to make every moment of every day.

So why am I prattling on about God and enlightenment in this book about animals? Because it might take reconnecting with your truest, highest, authentic divine self to regard animals differently than the way you have up until now. To be willing to see what eating them, wearing them, and using them for entertainment really is. When the egoic desire for meat, a pair of shoes, or seeing your kids happy has its death-grip on your psyche, this remembrance of who you are—who you *really* are—might be the only way to help you stop hurting animals.

That we even need to be reminded not to harm animals is a testament to how far we've gotten from our godliness. I don't say this with arrogance, like I think I'm godly now because I'm vegan. The animal issue was easy enough for me to grasp, but I've forgotten my innate godliness in so many ways. One of them was language. I've been using really profane language my whole life. It only occurred to me recently that I'm not serving myself or others by swearing. Yes, it can be funny. Really funny. I was good at it. But today, being funny is less important to me. When I got really clear on how contaminated humanity already is with profanity, promiscuity, ego, and duality, I knew that I did not want to add any more toxicity to the world. If I wish to be part of an enlightened humanity, I need to speak in a more conscientious and virtuous way.

So I'm speaking to you honestly and earnestly and trying to address the highest common denominator—the divine seed in your heart. The part of you that maybe lies dormant, but is stirred by truth and beauty and the chance for elevated spirit. The part of you that you might not have known existed but is quickening now with an ancient remembrance. The true you.

I love how spiritual teacher and Jain leader, Gurudev Shri Chitrabhanuji defines it: "Dharma means to be in one's original nature—the state an object will return to when not influenced from the outside. For example, the nature of water is to remain cool. You can boil it and it will become hot, however, when you put it down, after a while it will become cool again."[412]

So, what's your dharma? What's your original nature? Even if your whole life has seemed like a hedonistic, selfish, meaningless existence, it doesn't mean it's who you really are. You can always come back to your original nature of goodness, kindness, compassion, and godliness. "Two Wolves" is a beautiful Cherokee parable that speaks to this inner struggle: An old Cherokee chief was teaching his grandson about life. "A fight is going on inside me," he said to the boy. "It is a terrible fight and it is between two wolves. One is evil—he is anger, envy, sorrow, regret, greed, arrogance, self-pity, guilt, resentment, inferiority, lies, false pride, superiority, self-doubt, and ego. The other is good—he is joy, peace, love, hope, serenity, humility, kindness, benevolence, empathy, generosity, truth, compassion, and faith. This same fight is going on inside you, and inside every other person, too." The grandson thought about it for a minute and then asked his grandfather, "Which wolf will win?" The old chief simply replied, "The one you feed."[413]

HOLY SHIFT

I wasn't born vegan. Until I had that moment of awakening, I was contributing to a lot of violence and suffering. And I'd be remiss if I didn't remind you, with love, that you too have been complicit in the confinement, torture, and slaughter of animals. Every time you ate one, wore one, went to the zoo or circus, bought one from a pet store, watched one on TV or in movies, or bought a product that used one in their advertising. You may not have been doling out the actual abuse, but you weren't far removed at all—just far enough to not feel guilty.

As Oprah says, quoting Maya Angelou, "When we know better, we do better." So now you know better. Will you do better? Who are you *now*, in this very moment? Will you close this book, be sad or angry about the abuse that animals endure, and then eat chicken tonight? I don't ask this with anger or judgment; I ask it with love. I really do. I know that change is difficult. Painful, even. But if you can't control your own impulses that have you eating animals or buying their skins, then how do you expect those much worse off than you to control the impulses that have them harming or exploiting animals? Gandhi famously said, "Be the change you wish to see in the world." If we want a kinder, more loving, and compassionate world, then we each need to be kinder, more loving, and compassionate.

I love the Buddhist notion of *Bodhisattvas*—awakening beings. In his book, *Awakening the Buddha Within*, Lama Surya Das says that, "A Bodhisattva is someone with pure, impeccable intentions—a gentle yet fearless spiritual warrior who strives unceasingly to help everyone reach nirvanic peace and enlightenment." I'm not Buddhist, but I like the idea of being a peaceful warrior. There's a Bodhisattva Vow, that Das says, "The moment you affirm that great intention—to work for the good of all living creatures—whether or not you are always able to follow it as perfectly as you might wish—you are called a Bodhisattva, a child of the Buddhas." And that when we take this vow, "to realize enlightenment and relieve universal suffering, all the Buddhas, Bodhisattvas, devas, angels, and guardians of the Dharma clap their hands and rain down celestial flowers and divine nectar. It's like you scored a touchdown or hit a home run." I'm not sure we get to call ourselves Bodhisattvas if we don't take the vow, but we can certainly all try to be soldiers of love. And when faced with deciding between your old ways and a new way, it couldn't hurt to imagine all those celestial beings rejoicing every time you choose compassion and love.

I think one of the best soldiers of love was Dr. Martin Luther King Jr. His passion for righteousness was on par with his positivity that it was imminent. "When our days become dreary with low-hovering clouds of despair, and when our nights become darker than a thousand midnights, let us remember that there is a creative force in this universe, working to pull down the gigantic mountains of evil, a power that is able to make a way out of no way and transform dark yesterdays into bright tomorrows. Let us realize the arc of the moral universe is long but it bends toward justice." It bends toward justice. Amen.

Let us pray. Let us pray for the animals who suffer so deeply. Let us pray for the people who harm them, consciously and unconsciously. And let us pray for the collective consciousness to shift—that as a race, we never use, harm, or exploit animals ever again.

But first and foremost, let us each pray for our own inner strength, that all of our choices reflect the compassion etched in our hearts. "The Serenity Prayer," popularized by Alcoholics Anonymous, says it perfectly: "God, grant me the strength to accept the things I cannot change, the courage to change the things I can, and the wisdom to know the difference."

May you be courageous enough to change.

"If we do not act, we shall surely be dragged down the long, dark and shameful corridors of time reserved for those who possess power without compassion, might without morality, and strength without sight."

—Dr. Martin Luther King Jr.

"We are the ones we have been waiting for!"

—The Hopi Elders

ACKNOWLEDGMENTS

Brilliant, funny, fun Laura Dail: you are—bar none—the *best* literary agent. I'm so thankful for your endless patience, humor, wisdom, and savvy.

I'm not sure I would've written this book if not for NBC's Peter Costanzo. Thank you, Peter, for coaxing me out of hibernation with your steadfast support and enthusiasm.

Immense gratitude to everyone at Running Press and Perseus Books for investing so much time, energy, care, and hard work. Special and heartfelt thanks to:

- Jennifer Kasius, for that first "yes" (in a sea of "nos") all those years ago and all the "yeses" since; all your talent and skill; and your committed attention to every detail.

- David Steinberger, for your faith and benevolence.

- Chris Navratil, for the hands-on help and careful consideration.

- Allison Devlin and Seta Zink, for cooking up clever ways to spread *Beg* far and wide.

- Clay Farr and Jaimee Callaway, for e-planning and -plotting in the digital galaxy.

- Josh McDonnell, for making a beautiful finished product and all the work it took along the way.

- Joelle Herr, for your meticulous copyediting.

- Julie Ford, for being a force for good in the fight against evil.

- The amazing sales reps, who make sure all our hard work is not for naught.

Thank you Justin Loeber, Patrick Paris, Kristen Huff, and Bryana Curtis at Mouth Public Relations for working hard, smart, and with integrity. It's obvious you care about a job well done, and it's comforting to be in such good hands. The same goes for Rusty Shelton and the team at Shelton Interactive.

One of the many benefits of being a member of an animal loving community is the boundless goodwill of others. For your wise counsel and kind help, I thank you: Jonathan Balcombe, Gail Eisnitz, Lisa Lange, Julia Gallucci, Dan Paden, Bruce Wieland, Aryenish Birdie, Patti Howard, Kristie Sullivan, Dr. Neal Barnard, Nathan Runkle, Ian Elwood, Lisa Franzetta, Kathryn Levy, Phillip Rosen, and Glenn Berkenkamp. For our precious cover model and perfect animal ambassador, thank you Sylvia Elzafon. Blake Gardner, thank you for capturing my fur family and me for our author photo.

For your wealth of knowledge and overwhelming generosity, bless you Bruce Friedrich, Justin Goodman, John Pippin, Paul Shapiro, and Lisa Bloom. I'd be embarrassed by your charity if it wasn't for the animals.

It takes a village to raise a dog, and my dogs have the most loving village in the wold. With love and gratitude, Timber, Joey, and Lucy wish to thank Reggie and Gina, Jenny Emerick, Cyndee and Joe Magnani, Blake Gardner, and Gina Walter. Lucy wants to especially thank her angel, Jane Garrison, for rescuing her. (Timber and Joey have nothing to say to Jane.)

I am blessed to come from a family of animal lovers. I'd like to thank my parents, Rick and Meri Freedman, for being my first examples and teachers of kindness and compassion. That you jumped into this movement with such fervor is a testament to your huge hearts and morality. I am so proud of you both. (Mom, bless you and thank you for the gnarly proof-reading.) Auntie M, thank you for the constant love and care. Lesley, Tim, and Maya Bailey: I love you dearly.

For your life-altering friendship, love, support, help, teachings, and guidance that impacted me and, as a result, this book, thank you: Tracy Silverman-Mednik, Lauren Silverman-Simon, Sue Jakinovich, Christine Santoro, Bernie S., Juan and Ciela, Josh Radnor, Caroline Horton, y toda la familia.

Friends and fellow activists—I can't imagine this world without you. Thank you for putting animals before yourselves, for being vegan, for spreading the love, and for reminding me that the world is good and that there's hope. Thank you for working for animals, volunteering, donating, petitioning, protesting, leafletting, emailing, posting, sharing, and caring. Thank you for rescuing, sheltering, fostering, and adopting. Thank you for being animal lovers.

For my beloved vegan friends who have become my family: you have filled my life with fun, love, laughter, and kale. I love you madly.

NOTES

1 www.aspca.org/about-us/faq/pet-statistics.aspx

2 www.aspca.org/about-us/faq/pet-statistics.aspx

3 Ibid.

4 www.aspca.org/pet-care/spayneuter/spay-neuter-top-ten.aspx

5 www.oxfordpets.com/index.php?option=com_content&view=article&id=61&Itemid=63

6 www.aspca.org/about-us/faq/pet-statistics.aspx

7 www.aspca.org/Fight-Animal-Cruelty/puppy-mills/puppy-mill-faq

8 www.cesarsway.com/dogbehavior/basics/10-Interesting-Facts-About-Bulldogs

9 www.nytimes.com/2011/11/27/magazine/can-the-bulldog-be-saved.html?pagewanted=all

10 Ibid.

11 roomfordebate.blogs.nytimes.com/2010/02/17/feeling-guilty-about-your-purebred-dog

12 www.petmd.com/dog/care/evr_dg_ear_cropping_is_it_right_for_your_dog#.

13 www.petplace.com/dogs/ear-cropping/page1.aspx

14 www.pawproject.org/declaw-surgery

15 Dr. Christianne Schelling, www.declawing.com

16 www.aspca.org/about-us/faq/pet-statistics.aspx

17 HSUS State Pound Seizure Laws, August 2012

18 www.peta.org/features/Utah-Labs.aspx

19 beaglefreedomproject.org/about

20 Madhusree Mukerjee, "Speaking for the Animals: A Veterinarian Analyzes the Turf Battles That Have Transformed the Animal Laboratory," *Scientific American*, August 2004. pp. 96-7

21 Justin Goodman, Director of Laboratory Investigations, People for the Ethical Treatment of Animals. Interview July 24, 2012.

22 www.peta.org/issues/animals-used-for-experimentation/animal-testing-101.aspx

23 www.peta.org/issues/animals-used-for-experimentation/animal-experiments-overview.aspx

24 www.peta.org/issues/animals-used-for-experimentation/animals-in-laboratories.aspx

25 Ibid.

26 Interview with Aryenish Birdie, Research Associate at Physicians Committee for Responsible Medicine, September 20, 2012.

27 www.peta.org/issues/animals-used-for-experimentation/Smoking-Experiments-on-Animals/Smoking-Experiments-on-Animals.aspx

28 www.pmi.com/eng/research_and_development/pages/animal_testing.aspx

29 www.pcrm.org/media/online/dec2010/monkeys-dosed-with-narcotics-addiction-experiment

30 The Need for Revision of Pre-Market Testing

The Failure of Animal Tests of COX-2 Inhibitors

John J. Pippin, M.D., F.A.C.C. FDA Open Public Hearing

Arthritis Advisory Committee Drug Safety and Risk Management Advisory Committee

February 17, 2005.

31 www.fda.gov/NewsEvents/Newsroom/PressAnnouncements/2006/ucm108576.htm

32 Marlene Simmons, et al., "Cancer-Cure Story Raises New Questions," Los Angeles Times, May 6, 1998. http://community.seattletimes.nwsource.com/archive/?date=19980506&slug=2749152

33 Jarrod Bailey, "An Assessment of the Role of Chimpanzees in AIDS Vaccine Research," Alternatives to Laboratory Animals 36 (2008): 381–428.

34 N. Bhogal and R. Combes, "TGN1412: Time to change the paradigm for the testing of new pharmaceuticals," ATLA 34 (2006): 225–239.

35 Ibid.

36 Ibid.

37 M. J. H. Kenter and A. F. Cohen, "Establishing risk of human experimentation with drugs: lessons from TGN1412" *The Lancet*, Volume 368, Issue 9544, Pages 1387 - 1391, 14 October 2006

38 E. J. Topol, "Failing the public health—rofecoxib, Merck, and the FDA," *New England Journal of Medicine*, 351 (2004): 1707–09.

39 D. J. Graham, D. Campen, R. Hui, et al., "Risk of acute myocardial infarction and sudden cardiac death in patients treated with cyclo-oxygenase 2 selective and non-selective non-steroidal anti-inflammatory drugs: nested case-control study." *The Lancet*, 365 (2005): 475–81.

40 B. O. Roep, M. Atkinson, and M. von Herrath, "Satisfaction (not) guaranteed: re-evaluating the use of animal models of type 1 diabetes," Nature *Reviews Immunology* 4 (2004): 989–97.

41 C. H. Tator, "Review of treatment trials in human spinal cord injury: issues, difficulties, and recommendations," Neurosurgery, 59 (2006): 957–87.

42 M. Macleod, "What can systematic review and meta-analysis tell us about the experimental data supporting stroke drug development?," International Journal of Neuroprotection and Neuroregeneration, 1(3) (2005): 201.

43 Email from John J. Pippin, M.D., F.A.C.C., director of academic affairs for the Physicians Committee for Responsible Medicine, December 14, 2012.

44 J. J. Pippin, "The madness in the method," *Science & Technology* 1 (2008): 171–74.

45 Ibid.

46 R. A. J. Matthews, "Medical progress depends on animal models—doesn't it?" Journal of the Royal Society of Medicine, 101 (2008): 95–8.

47 J. J. Pippin, 171–74.

48 Interview with Bruce Friedrich, Farm Sanctuary, Senior Director for Strategic Initiatives , November 29, 2012.

49 www.peta.org/issues/Animals-in-Entertainment/animal-actors-command-performances.aspx

50 articles.latimes.com/2008/aug/27/entertainment/et-brief27

51 Ibid.

52 Ibid.

53 Ibid.

54 Ibid.

55 http://aldf.org/downloads/95_animalsadvocatespring06.pdf

56 aldf.org/article.php?id=242

57 http://aldf.org/downloads/95_animalsadvocatespring06.pdf

58 http://aldf.org/downloads/95_animalsadvocatespring06.pdf

59 http://aldf.org/downloads/95_animalsadvocatespring06.pdf

60 http://aldf.org/downloads/95_animalsadvocatespring06.pdf

61 http://aldf.org/article.php?id=2044 articles.latimes.com/2008/aug/27/entertainment/et-brief27

62 Interview with Julia Gallucci, M.S., Primatologist, May 30, 2012

63 http://articles.latimes.com/2008/aug/27/entertainment/et-brief27

64 Ibid.

65 Ibid.

66 Ibid.

67 www.peta.org/issues/animals-in-entertainment/animal-actors-command-performances.aspx

68 articles.latimes.com/2008/aug/27/entertainment/et-brief27

69 www.peta.org/issues/animals-in-entertainment/animal-actors-command-performances.aspx

70 www.americanhumanefilmtv.org/archives/movies/mr.php?fid=7893

71 Ibid.

72 Email from American Humane Association, November 13, 2012.

73 www.cbsnews.com/2100-207_162-2118670.html

74 abcnews.go.com/blogs/entertainment/2012/03/hbo-luck-series-to-end-after-third-horse-dies-on-set

75 www.hollywoodreporter.com/heat-vision/peter-jackson-denies-hobbit-animal-392242

76 www.variety.com/article/VR1118062390

77 boxofficemojo.com/studio/?view2=yearly&view=company&p=.htm

78 www.peta.org/issues/animals-In-entertainment/elephants-broken-spirits.aspx

79 Ibid.

80 www.mnn.com/home-blog/guest-columnist/blogs/the-circus-elephant-in-the-room

81 Ibid.

82 www.youtube.com/watch?v=Cb_m-YZ1wgk

83 www.peta.org/issues/animals-In-entertainment/elephants-broken-spirits.aspx

84 www.peta.org/issues/animals-in-entertainment/circuses-USDA-citations-problems.aspx

85 Ibid.

86 www.peta.org/issues/animals-in-entertainment/circuses.aspx

87 Ibid.

88 Ibid.

89 www.mercyforanimals.org/zoos.asp

90 www.peta.org/issues/animals-in-entertainment/wildlife-parks.aspx

91 www.mercyforanimals.org/zoos.asp

92 www.peta.org/issues/animals-in-entertainment/zoos.aspx

93 Ibid.

94 Ibid.

95 www.mercyforanimals.org/zoos.asp

96 Ibid.

97 Ibid.

98 Ibid.

99 circuswatchwa.org/zoochosis.htm

100 www.mercyforanimals.org/zoos.asp

101 www.peta.org/issues/animals-in-entertainment/zoos-pseudo-sanctuaries.aspx

102 www.peta.org/issues/animals-in-entertainment/zoos.aspx

103 www.guardian.co.uk/world/feedarticle/10125032

104 www.peta.org/issues/animals-in-entertainment/zoos.aspx

105 Ibid.

106 Ibid.

107 Ibid.

108 www.mercyforanimals.org/zoos.asp

109 Ibid.

110 www.peta.org/issues/animals-in-entertainment/zoos.aspx

111 www.sharkonline.org/?P=0000000680

112 Ibid.

113 www.peta.org/issues/animals-in-entertainment/rodeos.aspx

114 Ibid.

115 Ibid.

116 www.banhdc.org/archives/ch-fact-reasons-6-4-11.shtml

117 Ibid.

118 Ibid.

119 Ibid.

120 Ibid.

121 Ibid.

122 Ibid.

123 Ibid.

124 www.mediapeta.com/peta/PDF/Horse_Drawn_Carriage_Factsheet_10-12-2010.pdf

125 Ibid.

126 www.peta.org/issues/animals-in-entertainment/horse-drawn-carriages.aspx

127 www.grey2kusa.org/about/index.html

128 www.aspca.org/fight-animal-crueltygreyhound-racing-faq.aspx

129 www.grey2kusa.org/about/index.html

130 www.aspca.org/fight-animal-cruelty/greyhound-racing-faq.aspx

131 www.grey2kusa.org/action/states.html

132 www.peta.org/features/suffering-dogs-used-in-iditarod.aspx

133 www.peta.org/issues/animals-in-entertainment/horse-racing.aspx

134 www.peta.org/issues/animals-in-entertainment/hunting.aspx

135 www.idausa.org/facts/hunting.html

136 Ibid.

137 www.peta.org/issues/animals-in-entertainment/hunting.aspx

138 www.idausa.org/facts/hunting.html

139 Ibid.

140 www.peta.org/living/animal-friendly-fun/deer-car-collisions-increase-during-hunting-season.aspx

141 Ibid.

142 www.peta.org/issues/animals-in-entertainment/hunting.aspx

143 www.idausa.org/facts/hunting.html

144 Ibid.

145 Ibid.

146 www.peta.org/living/animal-friendly-fun/deer-car-collisions-increase-during-hunting-season.aspx

147 Ibid.

148 www.idausa.org/facts/hunting.html

149 Ibid.

150 Ibid.

151 www.peta.org/issues/animals-in-entertainment/hunting.aspx

152 Ibid.

153 Ibid.

154 Ibid.

155 Ibid.

156 Ibid.

157 Ibid.

158 Ibid.

159 Ibid.

160 www.peta.org/issues/animals-in-entertainment/fishing.aspx

161 www.mercyforanimals.org/fish/fish-feel-pain.aspx

162 Ibid.

163 J. P. Balcombe, *Pleasurable Kingdom: Animals and the Nature of Feeling Good* (London: Macmillan, 2006), 185–86.

164 www.peta.org/issues/animals-in-entertainment/fishing.aspx

165 www.farmsanctuary.org/learn/someone-not-something/fish

166 www.peta.org/issues/animals-in-entertainment/fishing.aspx

167 Ibid.

168 Ibid.

169 Ibid.

170 Ibid.

171 http://blogs.scientificamerican.com/extinction-countdown/2012/07/18/hong-kong-imported-10-million-kilograms-shark-fins/

172 www.amcs.org.au/default2.asp?active_page_id=516

173 news.nationalgeographic.com/news/travel-news/2012/02/120210-shark-attacks-deaths-fatalities-science

174 www.amcs.org.au/default2.asp?active_page_id=516

175 www.peta.org/issues/animals-used-for-clothing/wool-fur-and-leather-hazardous-to-the-environment.aspx

176 Ibid.

177 www.peta.org/issues/animals-used-for-clothing/global-leather-trade.aspx

178 Ibid.

179 Ibid.

180 Ibid.

181 Ibid.

182 Ibid.

183 Ibid.

184 www.peta.org/issues/animals-used-for-clothing/leather-and-factory-farming.aspx

185 www.worstpolluted.org/2011-report.html, 34–37

186 Ibid.

187 Ibid.

188 Ibid.

189 Ibid.

190 Ibid.

191 www.peta.org/issues/animals-used-for-clothing/wool-fur-and-leather-hazardous-to-the-environment.aspx

192 Ibid.

193 www.peta.org/issues/animals-used-for-clothing/down-and-silk-birds-and-insects-exploited-for-fabric.aspx

194 Ibid.

195 www.peta.org/issues/animals-used-for-clothing/inside-the-wool-industry.aspx

196 www.peta.org/issues/animals-used-for-clothing/wool-industry.aspx

197 Ibid.

198 www.hsi.org.au/?catID=1179

199 Ibid.

200 Ibid.

201 www.peta.org/issues/animals-used-for-clothing/wool-industry.aspx

202 www.peta.org/issues/animals-used-for-clothing/inside-the-wool-industry.aspx

203 Ibid.

204 Environmental Change Institute, "Annual Review 2006," University of Oxford, 2006. 26

205 Simon Worrall, "Land of the Living Wind," National Geographic January 2004. http://ngm.nationalgeographic.com/print/features/world/south-america/argentina/wind-text

206 U.S. Department of Agriculture National Agricultural Statistics Service, "Agricultural Chemical Usage: 2000 Sheep and Sheep Facilities," May 2001. 4–11

207 Graham Rutt, "A Summary of Investigations of Sheep Dip Pollution in Southwest Wales 2002–2004," Environment Agency, 2005. 15

208 "Animal 'Fart Tax' Puts Wind Up New Zealand Farmers," Agence France-Presse, June 2003. http://www.dailytimes.com.pk/default.asp?page=story_22-6-2003_pg9_4

209 www.adaptt.org/killcounter.html

210 Ibid.

211 Ibid.

212 www.chooseveg.com/pigs.asp

213 Ibid.

214 Ibid.

215 www.peta.org/issues/animals-used-for-food/pigs-intelligent-animals-suffering-in-factory-farms-and-slaughterhouses.aspx

216 Ibid.

217 Interview with Bruce Friedrich, Farm Sanctuary, Senior Director for Strategic Initiatives, November 29, 2012.

218 www.chooseveg.com/pigs.asp

219 Ibid.

220 www.peta.org/issues/animals-used-for-food/pigs-intelligent-animals-suffering-in-factory-farms-and-slaughterhouses.aspx

221 www.huffingtonpost.com/bruce-friedrich/does-eating-meat-support-_b_773166.html

222 Ibid.

223 Hormel Foods Newsroom: Hormel Foods Position on Humane Handling, September 17, 2008.

224 www.humanesociety.org/animals/pigs/pigs_more.html#

225 www.peta.org/issues/Animals-Used-for-Food/pigs-intelligent-animals-suffering-in-factory-farms-and-slaughterhouses.aspx

226 Ibid.

227 www.peta.org/issues/animals-used-for-food/pigs.aspx

228 Eisnitz, Gail A. *Slaughterhouse: The Shocking Story of Greed, Neglect, and Inhumane Treatment Inside the U.S. Meat Industry*. Amherst: Prometheus Books, 2007, 125.

229 Ibid., 102.

230 Interview with Bruce Friedrich, Farm Sanctuary, Senior Director for Strategic Initiatives. November 29, 2012.

231 Ibid.

232 www.hsa.org.uk/Information/Slaughter/Pig%20Slaughter.html

233 www.peta.org/issues/animals-used-for-food/pigs-intelligent-animals-suffering-in-factory-farms-and-slaughterhouses.aspx

234 Eisnitz, Gail A. *Slaughterhouse: The Shocking Story of Greed, Neglect, and Inhumane Treatment Inside the U.S. Meat Industry*. Amherst: Prometheus Books, 1997, book jacket.

235 Eisnitz, Gail A. *Slaughterhouse: The Shocking Story of Greed, Neglect, and Inhumane Treatment Inside the U.S. Meat Industry*. Amherst: Prometheus Books, 2007, 84.

236 Ibid., 267.

237 Ibid., 133.

238 Ibid., 140–41.

239 www.farmsanctuary.org/learn/someone-not-something/110-2/

240 Ibid.

241 Ibid.

242 *Ninety-Five: Meeting America's Farmed Animals in Stories and Photographs*, edited by No Voice Unheard, published by No Voice Unheard, Santa Cruz, California, 2010, 57–8.

243 http://woodstocksanctuary.org/learn/factory-farmed-animals/cattle

244 Ibid.

245 Ibid.

246 Ibid.

247 Ibid.

248 Ibid.

249 Ibid.

250 Ibid.

251 Ibid.

252 www.farmsanctuary.org/the-sanctuaries/rescued-animals/featured-past-rescues/hurricane-katrina-in-the-wake-of-disaster-a-new-life-for-hundreds-of-chickens

253 timesdaily.com/stories/Dead-chickens-lost-pets-among-challenges,139069

254 woodstocksanctuary.org/learn/factory-farmed-animals/cows-for-dairy-new-version

255 www.chooseveg.com/dairy.asp

256 www.mercyforanimals.org/calves

257 Ibid.

258 www.chooseveg.com/dairy.asp

259 http://www.peta.org/issues/animals-used-for-food/cow-transport-slaughter.aspx

260 Eisnitz, 145.

261 www.law.cornell.edu/uscode/text/49/80502

262 www.peta.org/issues/animals-used-for-clothing/leather-and-factory-farming.aspx

263 Eisnitz, 132–3.

264 woodstocksanctuary.org/learn/factory-farmed-animals/cattle

265 www.upc-online.org/chickens/chickensbro.html

266 www.huffingtonpost.com/bruce-friedrich/does-eating-meat-support-_b_773166.html

267 Ibid.

268 articles.latimes.com/2012/nov/14/business/la-fi-mo-butterball-thanksgiving-turkey-abuse-20121114

269 www.huffingtonpost.com/bruce-friedrich/does-eating-meat-support-_b_773166.html

270 Ibid.

271 www.freakonomics.com/2011/11/22/artificial-insemination-what-about-the-other-animals

272 www.farmsanctuary.org/learn/someone-not-something/chickens

273 woodstocksanctuary.org/learn/factory-farmed-animals/chickens-for-eggs

274 Interview with Bruce Friedrich, Farm Sanctuary, Senior Director for Strategic Initiatives, November 29, 2012.

275 www.upc-online.org/chickens/chickensbro.html

276 www.peta.org/issues/animals-used-for-food/chicken-industry.aspx

277 Ibid.

278 Ibid.

279 www.peta.org/issues/animals-used-for-food/chickens.aspx

280 Ibid.

281 www.peta.org/issues/animals-used-for-food/chicken-industry.aspx

282 Ibid.

283 www.upc-online.org/chickens/chickensbro.html

284 www.peta.org/issues/animals-used-for-food/chicken-industry.aspx

285 woodstocksanctuary.org/learn/factory-farmed-animals/chickens-for-eggs

286 www.peta.org/issues/animals-used-for-food/chicken-industry.aspx

287 woodstocksanctuary.org/learn/factory-farmed-animals/chickens-for-meat

288 www.peta.org/issues/animals-used-for-food/chicken-industry.aspx

289 Ibid.

290 Ibid.

291 Ibid.

292 Ibid.

293 Interview with Bruce Friedrich, Farm Sanctuary, Senior Director for Strategic Initiatives, November 29, 2012.

294 Ibid.

295 www.upc-online.org/chickens/chickensbro.html

296 Ibid.

297 Interview with Bruce Friedrich, Farm Sanctuary, Senior Director for Strategic Initiatives, November 29, 2012.

298 woodstocksanctuary.org/learn/factory-farmed-animals/chickens-for-eggs

299 woodstocksanctuary.org/learn/factory-farmed-animals/chickens-for-eggs

300 www.upc-online.org/chickens/chickensbro.html

301 Interview with Paul Shapiro, Humane Society of the United States, Vice President, Farm Animal Protection, November 28, 2012.

302 woodstocksanctuary.org/learn/factory-farmed-animals/chickens-for-eggs

303 Ibid.

304 Ibid.

305 www.upc-online.org/chickens/chickensbro.html

306 woodstocksanctuary.org/learn/factory-farmed-animals/chickens-for-eggs

307 www.upc-online.org/chickens/chickensbro.html

308 Ibid.

309 www.peta.org/issues/animals-used-for-food/chickens.aspx

310 www.upc-online.org/chickens/chickensbro.html

311 woodstocksanctuary.org/learn/factory-farmed-animals/chickens-for-eggs

312 Ibid.

313 Ibid.

314 www.animalethics.org.uk/i-ch7-2-chickens.html

315 www.upc-online.org/chickens/chickensbro.html

316 Ibid.

317 http://www.upc-online.org/freerange.html

318 Ibid.

319 woodstocksanctuary.org/learn/the-humane-farming-myth

320 www.ams.usda.gov/AMSv1.0/pyprocessverifiedprograms "Official Listing of Approved USDA Process Verified Programs," accessed November 30, 2012, 1-7.

321 www.bloomberg.com/news/2010-11-30/perdue-farms-sued-over-humanely-raised-labeling-on-poultry.html

322 Ibid.

323 www.humanesociety.org/news/press_releases/2010/11/perdue_labels_112910.html

324 http://awionline.org/store/catalog/animal-welfare-publications/farm-animals/humanewashed-usda-process-verified-program-mi Rachel Matthews, "Humanewashed: USDA Process Verified Program Misleads Consumers About Animal Welfare Marketing Claims," March 2012, 2.

325 www.mercyforanimals.org/investigations.aspx

326 http://awionline.org/store/catalog/animal-welfare-publications/farm-animals/humanewashed-usda-process-verified-program-mi Rachel Matthews, "Humanewashed: USDA Process Verified Program Misleads Consumers About Animal Welfare Marketing Claims," March 2012, 2.

327 www.adaptt.org/killcounter.html

328 www.peta.org/issues/animals-used-for-food/fish-feel-pain.aspx

329 Ibid.

330 www.peta.org/issues/animals-used-for-food/hidden-lives-of-fish.aspx

331 www.telegraph.co.uk/science/science-news/3334295/Fast-learning-fish-have-memories-that-put-their-owners-to-shame.html

332 Ibid.

333 Ibid.

334 Ibid.

335 Ibid.

336 Ibid.

337 www.peta.org/issues/animals-used-for-food/commercial-fishing.aspx

338 Ibid.

339 Ibid.

340 www.greenpeace.org/usa/en/campaigns/oceans/threats/bycatch

341 www.peta.org/issues/animals-used-for-food/commercial-fishing.aspx

342 news.nationalgeographic.com/news/2005/06/0610_050610_dolphins.html

343 Ibid.

344 www.peta.org/issues/animals-used-for-food/commercial-fishing.aspx

345 news.nationalgeographic.com/news/2003/05/0515_030515_fishdecline.html

346 oardc.osu.edu/4850/Nearly-All-Ohioans-Concerned-About-Animal-Welfare.htm

347 Campbell, T. Colin, PhD, and Thomas M. Campbell II. *The China Study. Startling Implications for Diet, Weight Loss and Long-Term Health.* Dallas, TX: Benbella Books, 2006, 111.

348 Ibid.

349 Ibid., 115.

350 Ibid., 119.

351 Ibid.

352 Ibid., 218–19.

353 Ibid., 221.

354 Ibid., 147.

355 Ibid.

356 Ibid., 149.

357 Ibid.

358 www.nytimes.com/2012/03/13/health/research/red-meat-linked-to-cancer-and-heart-disease.html

359 Ibid.

360 Ibid.

361 www.huffingtonpost.com/kathy-freston/why-vegan-is-the-new-atki_b_114464.html

362 www.cancerproject.org/ask/eggs.php

363 Ibid.

364 www.peta.org/issues/animals-in-entertainment/fishing.aspx

365 Ibid.

366 Campbell, 178 and E Giovannucci, "Dietary influences of 1,25 (OH)^2 vitamin D in relation to prostate cancer," *Cancer Causes and Control* 9 (1998): 567–82.

367 Barnard, "Nutrition and Prostate Health," cancerproject.org. http://www.pcrm.org/search/?cid=3559

368 http://www.cdc.gov/cancer/prostate/

369 Campbell, 178.

370 Ibid., 161.

371 Ibid., 6.

372 www.pcrm.org/health/diets/vegdiets/health-concerns-about-dairy-products

373 Campbell, 205.

374 Ibid., 204.

375 Campbell, 7.

376 Ibid.

377 www.nytimes.com/2012/04/05/opinion/kristof-arsenic-in-our-chicken.html

378 abcnews.go.com/blogs/health/2012/07/11/superbug-dangers-in-chicken-linked-to-8-million-at-risk-women/

379 www.webmd.com/food-recipes/news/20110125/animal-farms-may-produce-superbugs?ecd=wnl_day_012611

380 www.nytimes.com/2012/04/05/opinion/kristof-arsenic-in-our-chicken.html

381 abcnews.go.com/blogs/health/2012/07/11/superbug-dangers-in-chicken-linked-to-8-million-at-risk-women

382 Eisnitz, 172.

383 Ibid.

384 Ibid., 173.

385 Ibid., 174.

386 Ibid., 175.

387 www.usatoday.com/news/health/2006-12-04-chicken-bacteria_x.htm

388 Campbell, 308.

389 Ibid.

390 Ibid., 91.

391 Ibid., 105.

392 Ibid., 94.

393 Ibid., 93.

394 Ibid., 103.

395 Ibid.

396 Ibid., 98.

397 www.earthsave.org/globalwarming.htm

398 www.professorshouse.com/Food-Beverage/Topics/Vegetables/Articles/Why-Become-a-Vegetarian

399 www.earthsave.org/globalwarming.htm

400 environment.nationalgeographic.com/environment/freshwater/embedded-water

401 Ibid.

402 www.pbs.org/now/shows/250/meat-packing.html

403 www.hrw.org/en/reports/2005/01/24/blood-sweat-and-fear

404 Ibid.

405 Ibid.

406 www.merriam-webster.com/dictionary/satori

407 www.yogananda-kriyayoga.org.uk/page8.htm

408 www.paloaltohumane.org/education/pdfs/How_safe_skies.pdf

409 Ibid.

410 www.peta.org/features/agriprocessors.aspx

411 www.happy-science.org/the-path-to-enlightenment

412 www.forbes.com/sites/michaeltobias/2012/09/18/a-jain-leader-addresses-the-world/

413 www.sapphyr.net/natam/two-wolves.htm

INDEX